MooNlight Howling

Poems from an existential anxiety attack

Emenual Wolff

To Matthew Swanson:
My eighth-grade English teacher, who said if he hadn't have sat behind me during class, he would've never believed it was really me who wrote it.

Eye becoming

First breath:

She had lived with that smell for most of her life;
    woodchips and mulch
    under metal swings and yellow
jungle gyms with red plastic roofs.
    With
grass stains, and bark from the long field
of her third-grade recess,
and the rubber of soccer balls.
The smell of what's archaic,
        the intensity of vitality,
            the few whiffs of wishful
moments
            serene, and steady moving,
              like the clouds of a
partial day.
She had lived with that sound,
the sound of most of her life:
    laughter, hollering over the chirping
    of plump, red bottomed birds;
everything trying to mate, to survive, to grow –
but not her, or the fluttering of her moths,
the spindling of her spider webs,
or the cries of her classmates.
She was simply just alive, with no inquiry.
No understanding of judgement, nor reason
of why the flowers closed up at night.
She assumed it was to shelter themselves from
morning dew, which always found its way down
    from the mountain, and back up again.
She assumed it was to go to church, and listen

to what whims of God, Jehovah.
She assumed he'd have the final call of judgement,
and trusted fully her mother would always
      have the answer. Even the answers
she didn't want to hear.

They were always given so delicately at first, it seemed,
like she was a special student.
A memorable rarity, individual in the
impressions and moments she'd birth to all
the other elders.
Their eyes eager,
so hopeful,
and looking down
confidently that she was an angel
of the future…
as if every analogy,
and all the models her tongue would
decorate were hung by God himself.
So, she was confused when she took her first breath
out of Eden. Because with it came question.
With it came inconclusions, unnatural, unfamiliar.
Like powerful ulcers in her mind of delusions -
though admirable, still peculiar.
And with it came authority, and splendor,
morality and gender,
and with his hazel blue eyes
he began to see the world in patterns –
cyclic design;
he birthed, once more.
he began to think
in rhyme.

Matthew 24:8

Evolution isn't quick, even if it is conscious.
It's a slumbering bears year being born,
torn from hibernation.
disoriented by the light, stumbling though cautious,
until it mumbles out of its cave and stands
in full liberation.
Good morning new world!
This new world with no answers,
built by a God with no beginning, for questions of
no end.
I found a God in
Matthew 24:8
When you raised your hand again
and again
and again
like witnessing the abandonment of a teacher with
her classmate –
striving higher, and higher
to receive that commending "YES!"
Only instead for me, I asked the questions,
but it was always the wrong one again.
Again,
and again.

But so do the Stars:

Why gold?
Why not apples
or beanie babies;
these things are all sold
and we hunger for it –
like mad dogs with rabies –
like a Cujo of wall street,
we dig up a bone like
we forgot where we buried it.

It isn't that grand, it's got a
slight shimmer, but so do
the stars.

It's found in the land,
but our land has grown dimmer
for the transport of
rebellion,
and food that is rot.
The sexuality of a culture,
violently uninterested.
Apathetic anthropoids, delivering
the archaic dance of wealth,
rain, and an "American dream."

God bless the U.S.A
It's in him that we trust,
This unidentified. Soldier. of amnesty.
God,
who placed us here in
absence of permission,

and birthed us in the first place.

Only a Demiurge could place such high Value on gold.

Paradoxical Personhood:

Forest nest within your flesh,
to crackle life throughout;
the net -
Where twine pulls tight
upon what's risen,
and finds itself red and agape.
Eyes welt jaded vastness upon
their sockets' satellites...
I know I don't look it, so just trust what I
do;
a macabre joy,
a comforting melancholy,
spewed like rainbow tar
to submit this suffocation,
      by passing by.
A need to live,
a need to die.

You took a perfectly abled beast
and you gave it personhood.

After that, the rest
is history.

Blueprint (five haikus):

.

Crisp mist licks this bliss
That I have inherited.
Dream, infinitely.

.

Dew, silhouetted
On a lash, sprouted by pearls,
Which belonged to love.

.

Fire against night;
Vortex combustion dances,
While still eyes retain.

.

Reality does.
Eclipsed is enlightening
Initiation.

.

Spiraling in this;
An envelope of data.
Our work never ends

.

Get Out of bed:

Morning birds, flower blooms,
a day's new florescent blue,
and mother's madness smiles
in algae plumes.
What a *beautiful* day!
Toe tips tickling cool sands;
smoky ashes clean the hour glasses
in my hands….
This blankets beaches
circumvents to flank my eyes
with memory leaches.
Life is on rewind,
and I can't quite grasp or find this
last kiss
with fist
and the lessons that it teaches.
Hatch my lashes with images
of previous winter years.
Blizzards of crucifixions and
fears.
White out medications
and snow flake tears.
Good morning, mourning birds.
Float softly,
      little song bird.
Glisten your chimes along the droplets
my eyes bathe.
Write. My. Life.
For I am dancing along the
exhale of existence,
screaming silent sight from

my hearts deflation,
and witnessing the never
found between each note of yours
you christen.
Let my nest give way,
set my spirit ablaze,
until I can hear nevermore
this ugly sweet song you've made.

Advice:

Don't ever try to support something that you
physically can't.
You might think that later it'll pay off;
that you'll feel *good*.
Feel like you really "stepped up." "took
responsibility,"
"became your *OWN*"
and took care of your pops, your moms,
your family; it doesn't feel like that kid.
It. Doesn't. *Feel*.
like that.
It feels like anger, in the pit of your gut.
It feels like I could've been somebody…

And every day is just another day where
my joints hurt,
my knees and back hurt,
and I have to ask myself with every word
if it's even worth tellin' someone.

I tell you kid, don't get old.

In the Lead:

All the little martyrs, executed
lessons of lesser
life choices, or perhaps just a hesitation
of the jump. A flickering of surety,
once punctured by the envelope
of what's already been done
and known.
All the fearless failures
of yesterday's every day; they don't
show their badges until they're
long gone into
the photographs. All I know of
not to do, I know
from watching you, you flowers,
you poppies,
you flyers and followers of nothing –
you racers, and jumpers, and fires
of hunger, you saviors
unsaved.
Life is so strange, and
it plays for keeps.
The beast of an unforgiving "now,"
where indecision is the present tense
of regret.
Thank you,
*so **fucking** much*,
for going first.
I miss you, and I owe you my life.

I'm as Happy as a Pawn:

Hell
is left unfed,
flames unfelt;
for it to ash,
I offer myself unto this dawn.
Plastic lights, figurines,
toy trucks,
tractors, and limousines.
Colored pencils, beanie babies, notebooks, bibles
and magazines.
The slate blue carpet screams
sincerity
of absolute stone to etch
with memory.
A past sewn through red metal
twin mattress bunks, and silhouettes
of shadows in the dark.
Tick
tick
ticking from the hallway's
iridescent headlight window
blind art.
I don't know you, and
I lose my mind trying
to recollect implicitly.
I lose my mind in fractions
of distractions and
casualties.
Cartoons, pillow cases, buttons and
candies.

Teddy bears, bath soaps, fists and blue jeans.
Confusion, denial, delusion
and smiles under
slate blue eyes, under paper skin,
and high pitched cries under
contraband sin.

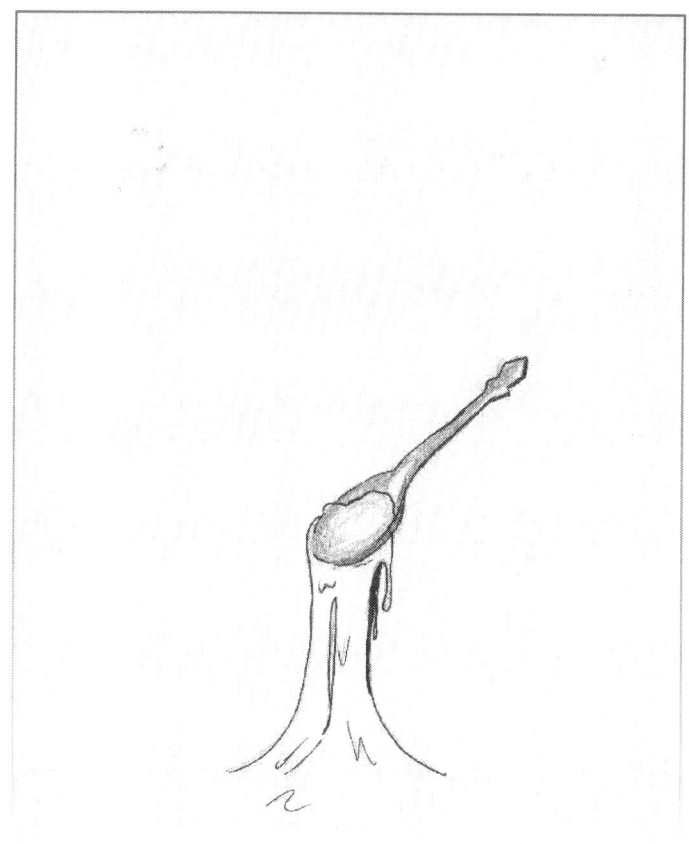

90's kids:

There's a sort of melancholiac magic
in the mediocrity of youth. Young adults who have way
too much are rotten; too little is
tragic.
In a happy medium exist this aura of vitality,
and a lazy tug of potential, always.
Topped off with a cherry of invincibility, just
waiting to be popped.
It's the way they flick the cigarette between
their lips. The way they nod hello, like
they're gonna be here for a while.
A laugh that's just a little forced,
because they know how good
it feels
to draw it out.
That's the magic of a youth with a finger print to leave
behind at the scene
of their own murder.

Happy birthday, kid.

Dracula:

How hallow a kiss, do
these eyes bliss;
these windows to a soul,
so careless, so diluted.
      For so too does it flow through
                           holograms unhinged;
              and so too do these bones
chew
                      through every nerve,
                    and sin –
                    every time,
and

    end.
What hallow cries, like mothers' skies,
Do we naturally give in.
                  I am the lie
         the spider-fly
         in this paradox I spin,
   and
    I won't die, these words are mine;
in each one, a new world
        begins.

A Right of Passage:

I am your lie, and   I
will always be here. I will always
see the dead in your eye.
As if we could ever grow tired of waiting;
as if we could ever grow tired of being
alive.

The gasp cut short so soon,
this transcending sigh. What does it mean
to have lived long enough to finally
feel
alive?

This silence and stare is
hysteria-violence compared to any answer
I've cried. I don't know;
I don't know what I'm supposed to do here.
I know of cosmos, and microscales,
and of biology still animal;
the natural
spirit fire that they bind. I know
of art, and love, and hope,
but I know nothing of your kind. There's
a whole world out there, spinning
around on life rewind, but
it's not the end of the world…
It's not the end of the world, the planet will be fine,
it's us who've lost all heart and mind.
Dog ear this page of yesteryears and
spit another layer
of dripping paint and scriptures

depicturing the trick –
the surface layer that we suck and lick to taste
the sugar, the milk and honey of a world
that isn't real, but we accept
with endearment,
a fond infatuation of the idol;
the lie.

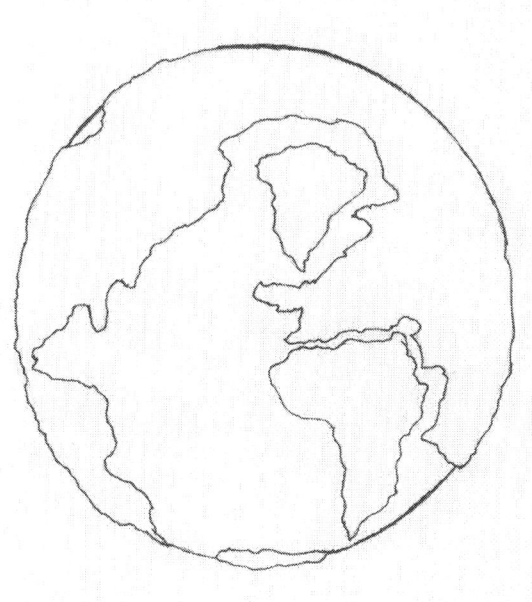

Forgiveness:

Show me eyes like scars
to sooth and seethe the thoughts
thrice far and smoothly breathe
        calm vision light – ajar and free,
this vision gift that's deep as dust,
and hard as feather leaves;
        sweet nectar light of lust and color
brilliance;
        this stroke of sights delivery.

        A spirits' night, laced with life so high,
unfolded like love,
        this peddled rose and dilated eye.
            Unfolded thoughts on heavy minds
        and stars as bright as thee.
            Collapse your judge's scarlet lies
        where harlot guilts do bed to see…
        Within the sockets void of time,
rest scar lit eyes to stare
                at me.

A High in Depth:

                         For our mother is most proud
when we return to her soil.

                                She turns
                 perpetually,
                 blue along her cosmic coil.
                        Dear mother, glow
pleased,

               I shall soon return

      to your soil.

FEAR:

Crackling chains pulled sharp
against teeth, worn dull
from chewing apart
the meat in my skull,
until black chains are burnt,
white walls are broken,
freedom well earnt
by a force misspoken.

Freedom, that which was never truly lost,
was never found to begin.
This force that pays with its own cost
will never truly end.
What's the toll of a bridge of bones
fueling their own fire?

These walls will always be torn,
serrated by rotten teeth
and dangling skin.
This force now reborn,
no longer makes me weak
enough to never give in.

The fear of fear makes the fearless
a tortured beast.
It breaks through white walls, the fear of fear
released.
Raised above,
in most ways deceased
I climbed up the wall where
it was fear I learned to love

…and still it's not enough.

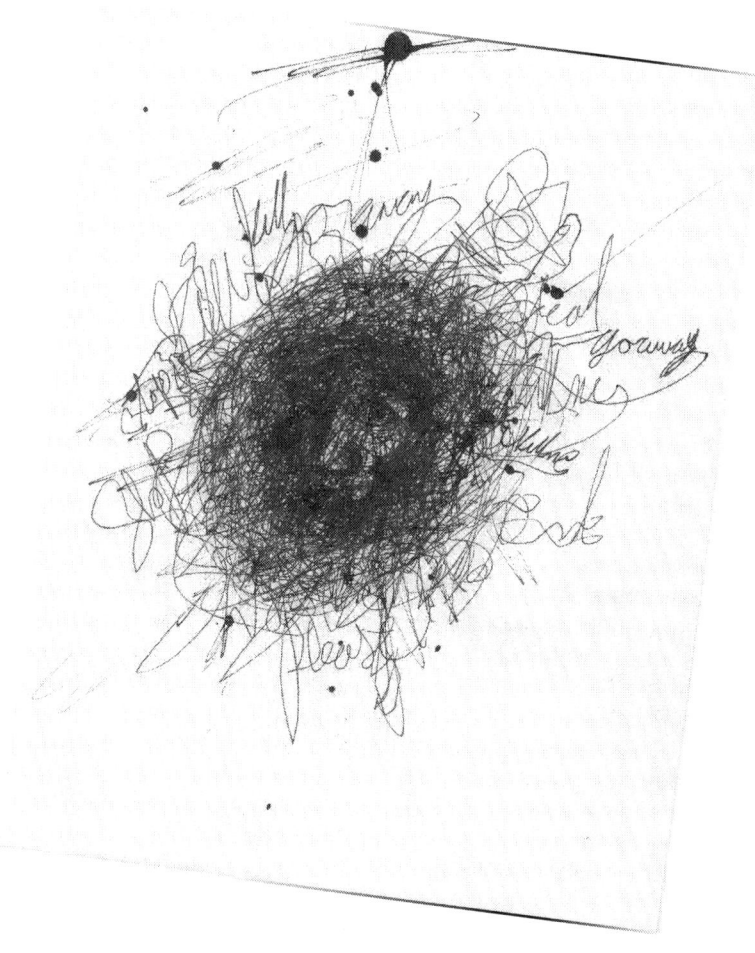

A Cloak:

So, answer me, please,
when I ask you this query;
what exactly do you expect from me?
What more could you expect to see?

Who was it who gave you such an endless
expectancy?

Who ruined you angel,
and forced your only solution to be vagary.
I loved you once child, and you to me.

What did I do
to turn you so
black?

Secrets:

I'd rather you hate me than be dead.
I pushed you under water, I

drowned you in your head.
I used you as desire,   drugged
you through my whispers,
and tirelessly dangled keys
above the words, I   said.

Just above your eye.
I let you say "I love you"
I let you say a lie.
I'm your friend,
your brother,
your lover,
your end.
I'm your moon,
your clear night cloud,
your evergreen.
        Sometimes, I'm you.

I'm older than language
with names, only the
dirt dare murmur.
I'm everything you've ever seen.
I'm everything we run.
You see child, the moon
will *always*
rain
the sun.

Cut Off:

Strings pulling strings in
        the inevitably burden – the
            blank space of the brain.
Casual chemical conjunction creates a catastrophe,
        a life with function,
            a natural calligraphy; *what*

am I to say I see, when all I can say are the words
you've taught me?
        Oh, of all the hell enabled by
you, this inherited vocabulary.
        A vernacular of disaster;
    a tight funnel drained for a beaker vile, a
lizard skinned sack of pain.

        With these thoughts, so potent, in a brain
so extraordinarily dull,
        so as to see things as they truly are,

it's a mystery,

        a blunder,

                I squander any real breath at all.

Discovering the Eyes:

Paint pains mirror along a highway's
predecessor.
Swirl a pictures vocabulary, delicately
the creator and editor.
We don't omit mistakes, we just…
cover them up;
we don't admit the fake face we use
to drink love in cups
of
scotch and powdered water.
Our blood we spill,
our earth we slaughter.

Sought love in daughters from
sons whose fathers abandoned them and
caught her.
<u>The loop.</u>
It flows in the eyes of minds who glow and
hearts that grow in cyclical order and entropy; and
so it goes…
and
so it goes…
twist spills, sipped ill thoughts seeding ends,
bleeding beginnings bended by the living.
Killed by their futures inevitable birth.

So, paint pleasure on paper –
Search your soul and try your hardest not to hate
her.
There isn't a now, but there's always a flow,
and a you, and a truth, to learn how to know.

Learn to Shut Your Mouth:

Stay light
softly on the silent ground.
A violent spite in pale nights found
the vile sight of umbilical's
bound on you like gravity.
Sound the alarms;
she groans again.
Stay silent as she lunges in
and shuts
the spirit down
within.
SOUND the ALARMS; he can't begin.
Stay silent as he plunges down
your head below the water;
sin.
Stay…
silent as long as you can stay
silent.
Softly until the end.

To Touch a Flame:

The past glares,
younger, sadder, beaten it
stares through the mirror –
how could you have let this happen?
An entity of naivety,
a snake of mistake slithering in;
its spine up mine
into the mud behind our eyes;
if for a moment to bridge
realization
with regret.
      The
dumbest thing I ever did,
now stands before my memories;
the dumbest version of me I see
and it's begging, *please*, to die.
For every time I've brought it to life
it catches fire, and *screams* till dry.
While I
alone
am wet to cry
of this ever-becoming endless eye.
Twenty-twenty hindsight
is a stapled screen
onto our mirrors and minds.
with abled screams
we sink into the dirt –
these sentient
tortured
flies.

Numb:

>
> I mean, just imagine
> if I couldn't feel…
>
> all the people I could be?
> Whomever you wanted,
> whatever you please;
> but for me. All for me.

INK:

This is a story, about a boy who's a number;
and a glass,
and a pill,
and a state of long slumber.
He can wear a smile, and is usually well dressed,
but the world made him dull, and his demons
depressed…

A world ruled by cash made us *slaves at our best*
and I know that it's rash, but this *burns* this boys' *chest*
and
his soul cried to know that it couldn't go home,
that his mind he couldn't own,
that his body was a drone,
this. <u>*Killed*</u>. Him.

…. well at least it almost did. Several times over
he could've died, just a kid.
but he didn't seem to die, and life became a prison
locked and chained by the sky
as everything below in his vision
was unveiled as a lie.
Time would beat by in a counter clockwise rotation,
repeating the steps taken in this
mind control
re-education, deindividuation station
where he'd loop around on his usual course,
chasing good grades,
getting fed data from an unilluminated source
knowing

full well that it could be out dated.
That he was probably only being bated
to have a *job*, not a life.
That he'd probably never even have a wife
or kids -
he's pushing buttons, pulling levers, just to get the pay to live.
He's reading text books, going class to class,
droning *on and on* with a name that'll never even last
in this
day of age
where you hardly learn a lesson you just
turn the page
to six-hundred and sixty-seven.
There's no moral compass in this *mess* between hell and heaven,
and sure, the bible's being sold like a dime a dozen but if
"God is our father, that makes Satan our cousin."

This does drive him crazy. His will to live grows lazy.
He's hazy
from waking up from a whole *lifetime* of pushing daises.

Nothing seemed to help the way he doesn't feel,
and like a hamster in his cage he just keeps....
...turning the wheel...

No, he couldn't find an outlet. But over again
he'd find his life at a reset.

And JUST as infinity was beginning to *bend*
his false sense of sanity;
as the lack of a flame was burning his divinity;
when he *knew* that an island like Earth had no lighting,
he was picked up and loved, by the goddess of writing.

See, he was always an artist, but his creations were dark
until the first time she found him
and ignited that spark underneath his skin.
As his heart would cry out, then *So. Would. His. Pen.*
Every sentence was a life-line, saving his soul.
Pulsing parabolic, phonetically twisting each phrase
in ways that could push or pull *any* agnostic.

He'd write out the thoughts that crawled from under his bed,
to set them free on blank paper,
to silence his head.
Soon he saw that this personified metaphor was exactly the kind of love
That he was looking for, to turn his spirit canine
whose howl could be heard.
He began to dream again,
to free his world
with the <u>weapon</u>
of written
word.

2
Medicinal Poison and Violent Catharsis

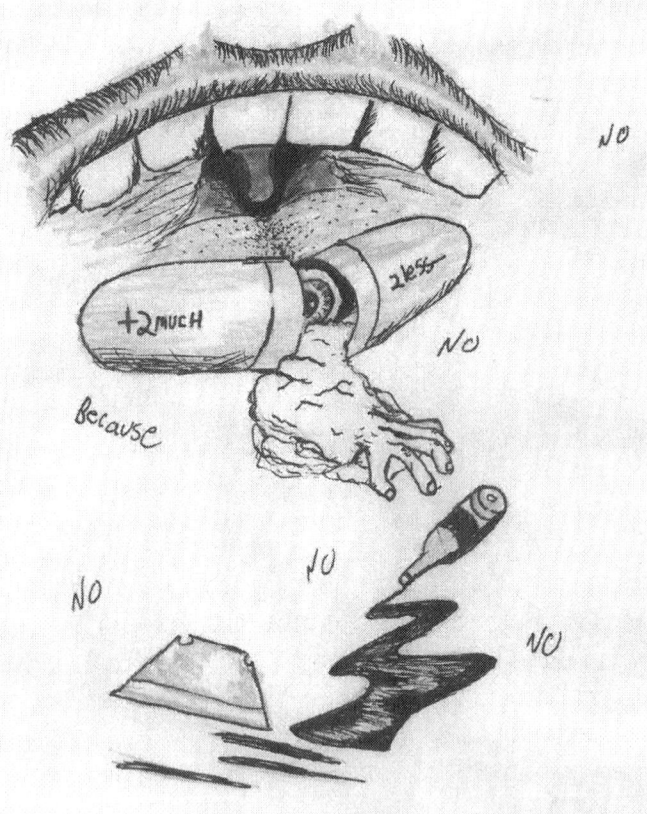

Charity:

I gave a man money, because he spoke with his palms,
and sincerity.
He didn't meet my eyes when he asked,
but I wouldn't have asked him to.
I don't know what's more shameful; a
broken records worth of "thank you's,"
or a single apology, no matter how
severe its sincerity.

She covers us all; the sky.
With lies and cries of atmospheric riddles
we ask *"why?"*
the smoke infects my minds – plural, yes,
like every cloud I breathe to seep drearily into the
highest tides of our fading
parting
skies.

I gave him money; I would've given him a ride.
I didn't know the man, but of that he didn't mind
when he approached to ask for whatever I had to
spare.
It could've been passive robbery, in fact
it most likely was,
and I knew, but I passionately didn't care.

Maybe we'll meet again, in a past or life next…
maybe…

Two clouds above us stayed perfectly parted from one another,
never to mix or merge and form a new pattern on their blue canvas.
Never to meet, but just strain out of reach,
for five, measly dollars.

Easy:

So much counting lately…
Counting parts,
counting days,
counting sets, reps,
and cash.
Counting drinks,
        counting pills
counting friends,
counting
how many   times
        you say you   love me.
            Counting hours,
        minutes,
     eternal seconds…

    Counting on

              the thought
that
any of this

            counts.

Smoke Temperaments:

Death is a salty lake
that sways with unconsciousness
and I
am clutching on to life
by a bottle and a fishing line.

I lost one of my better sides because
it feared I'd sink to suicide, but,
who am I to lie and try to decide whether or
not
they were right?
Puppet strings tie knots on my mind tonight,
but ultimately, it's my life that strides
the strife I fight.
Ultimately, it's my drink that
melts the ice I bite, and,
ultimately, it's not me
who guides the knife I spite over my skin
in shapes of sins I indulge my nostrils in.

     it's okay… because you tried your best, so
you deserve this break; take a breath.
There'll be plenty of room for space
when there's nothing of me
left.

Undesirable Organs:

I am the moon,
                I'm the sun,
and I swoon
who I sway,

and I smile,
'till it's done.

You trust what I say,
        until it's that
        of damages.
and
use me all day,
        as alcohol and
bandages.
It
isn't black,
        it's just silent.
        It thinks without *me* in
sex   drugs   and violence.
    Beat.   *Beat.*   *Beat.*

I Hope You Smile:

With eye lids dim, tolling your dial,
so begins your swim down our
powdered Nile.
I hope you *fucking smile*, like
I know you do too,
while she climbs you up!
One. More. Mile.
and *invades* the words you chew…
Hack into the heart, **Mutiny** your mind;
tear angels **apart** so *heaven* you may find.
Drink yourself to art, with
violent colored wine; pen
your ink onto the table –
do another line…
sedative psychedelic,
        relatively melancholic,
                collectively demonic spells
        spill tells of hell from our souls
    ceiling.
Go AHEAD, *write* the world
what you *think* you *might* be feeling.
Because it's a **salvation**, a
dedication to *creation*; it's ***not***.
healing.

Night Sharks in the Ocean:

Hand me a drink,
a couple pills,
paper link,
and some kind of fire
because

                ...

while you taste on the ceased play
of an eye that's grown tired,
I wish to haste the decay of a world
born ire.
I sip a glass built of iron
ore, for
bitter sweet inner sores,
all aboard and bored of
beach waves, flailing bridges to
evermore.
Drained in a song,
our mind dances in wires
made of sparks, and sparkling
chemical colliders, together
transiting along
the lips and life
of a liar.
Smile, though dull.
Eat, though full.
.

Push, just to pull….
.

Push, just to pull.

Mice and Kittens:

Lines of lust in
order of sin,
rushing my blood
of chemical kin.
Running back,
like mice to kittens –
– It was meant to be –
– like burning logs,
      cats and dogs,
and locks of linen:
      the deadly soft
           of subtle
stretches in pulse and vision
when you
grab vigorously,
      at biting euphoria.
Clench the blood pressure,
and the inside cheeks.
Clench at the stagnant, wasted
stimuli of the same
disgusting
human stained room you've
been in for weeks, screaming
your mind to quit *starving*
of happy.
      Do I dare peer out
into the burning day light,
      without the color of enzyme?
So it begins every time
I make it end;
my maze of mice and kittens.

Risen Skin:

My head is haunted;
I'm trashed,
       wet, and
              unwanted.
Droplets spill
       fever endorphins;
so red… so aesthetic.

The layer crawls beneath repeat
until I feel prosthetic.
A piece of meat.

       Water stings,
       but then it numbs.
My body's dead, my mind is dumb,
       as I wish to re-stitch my
itch – scratch.
       I thought my blood was black
so, I went searching for its hue.
       I cut the pain out from my chest,
and it turned up in you.
I've got nothing
left to lay to rest, and I've lost the tools to
prove, that I'm alive and life's worth
living with the pain you
send me through.

Itch – scratch.
As normal as a breath and
primal to detach;
discover coves of death in Zen. Make

a gun with two fingers,
pull the trigger,
again
and
again,
again and
again, because you
itch, scratch.
As quickly as the heart beat –
you penetrate in violence,
lusting agony milked from
repeated defeat.
Peel the scab – you itch,
scratch until you bleed.
Vomit secreting thoughts
that you only after
disagree.
Powdered ice sinks mutiny
– abandon ship – sip pain or exist –
cover the itch, and blacken your dismay.
You're drowning and air
is but a finger nail away.
Itch – scratch.

Vent:

Shatter splinters corner crash the glass
and aluminum indents.
2x4 justice on inanimate ancients.
Cars in a cobweb shed, and tequila jarred
head
ached
by secret polygamy.
I broke
And broke,
And broke the windshields like destiny.
Like destiny broke
my sex drive, my love, my
identity.
Like every promise that's been broken;
every comfort that's been stolen from me;
every aspect of my bullshit family.

Light a cigarette with the flame of revenge and
bible ink; gravity
takes control the moment I let go,
and sink into the velvet night. Behind the
orange curtain of aroused power;
within the trees and air they devour. Gravity
pulls me further and further
so naturally far away
from it all.
Instead of crawl I learned to fall
into the splinters
that stick in ponders, *"why?"*

Why:

Do you remember?
When I called with a
handful of pills,
ready to swallow the world, like
the way you ate my heart?
You forced me to chuck em' at snow
covered hills in my back yard,

and made me think

of the chills I still
get when I picture my little sister's eyes
being hit
by death dripping gurgling bubbles
out of my lips,
onto the rope,
…the morning after.
You saved my life in a single stroke.
Now look at you… taking the long
way home, to contemplate delusion prone
ideas of how *her* suicide could coincide with
overcoming fears.
At this point, you'd watch anything happen.
Why would
you have saved my life
if this
was who you
were going to become?

-Dear Lucy

Dive into live blue skies
that which holds clouded lies,
shrouded in the dark
Of what's broken; our heart

splits open
to sing its deadly melody.

She is my melody. She being the being, the witch
that which
brings me an overload of empathy,
if only for a moment,
bringing to
life that light that which beats the
pendulums rhythm within my chest.

She is the
feminine spirit,
resting in my pupils' moon;
that
which
I howl for her presence.
Come to me please, creativity.
Give me a reason to breathe
such sensitivity;
give to me sweet nectar Lucy
so I could lose my life
entirely
without the commitment.

Remedy:

Can't keep beating at this rate.
It feels like I've forgotten how to breathe.
It feels like parallel worlds are
are resting on my
ribs.
It feels, and
I don't want to feel anymore.

Press exit. Control alt delete,
and shut down.
Escape.
Escape…
Escape when gravity is distinguishable,
and the air is peculiarly dense.
When vision is warm and soft
as the black, breathing through the night,
but something seems *so. Wrong.*

This is where we are blanketed in mortality.

Snuggled up in the sheets of what's human,
Tucked within our after-hour interaction.
Sometimes we prey on the dead.
…I don't even remember her name…
The switch is of a righteous altercation;
a transit from one play ground to the next –
where vision is sharp and things like density
and gravity strike a lighter intensity,
but I magically feel like so much more.
God more…

more
more than anything do I feel I wish It'd worked...
Cut out my lungs...
I can't do it myself.
To so little and long I've clung
to this cognitive stealth, this
esteemed engine of sensation, sex, and game.
Staying above feathered waters, by
strings of mental
health.
End the program.
Cut it out.
Cut me out –

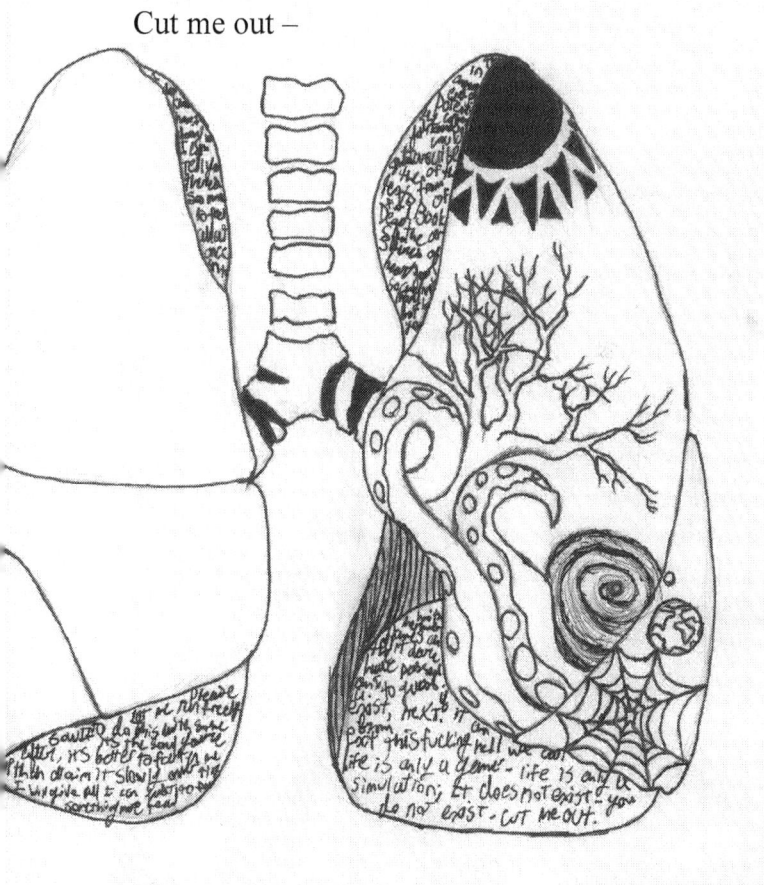

A Loop of Love:

My left side is your spit,
swinging from those thin, pale lips.
My right is the air,
squeezing together
as your eyes move closer to mine.

This mind is in shambles,
shattered by that needled kiss
and piercing augmented argument inside,
piecing
together exactly why
it was
my knees buckled.
My heart pumps backwards
as you lunge your arms around my bones.
Relapse,
relapse,
relapse, once more,
hold tight, and
don't let go. Become one;
bore
a future,
set in place by this moment,
flooding in your past.
The whole loop is present,
happening at once, as this wasn't your decision.
This wasn't your decision;
it's never been anything you could control,
accept for such an absolute center
as this.
perhaps,

to prolong with fear
as fuel; to last longer in
this planetary realm,
under our blanket of stars,
whose
 finger tips
   have reached down now,
     to let us merge in a fraction
   of our absolute,
and relapse once more.
          One, two, and three.
Feeling spiraling masses of glitter,
gold,
light,
and fire;
of will and power,
gravitationally pulling each other.
Too close to be two,
yet one mind would never do;
so, they toil in coils endlessly with godly reason,
confused as vines,
versed with divine imagination,
and color each other with the essence of their
reflections.
Existence perhaps,
in fluidic bits of particle-wave;
they pull with such persistence, chemically they
cave.
She remembers, he can see its name, in their three.

O.D:

Everyone I think I know,
including myself,
is not *afraid* to die. But
then it actually starts happening
                  and
you're like, "wow, am I about to
actually do this *shit **right now***?
I don't know… I mean, I had plans
for May…"

It's fucked,   completely.
We come to terms with the fact that we're
going
to die – one side of mortality – but it's different
than coming to terms with how we could easily die
at literally any other moment… the other side
of mortality. Because one… one is inevitable, and
it's

natural,
and it's a beautiful release; a titan motivator; a
formula for life, within its ceaseless cyclic nature;
while the other is just…

                  oh god

and it makes living kind of like a nightmare, the
more you focus on it. So, when you come
face to face with it, with dying young,
because of an idiotic misadventure at a house party
of opiates and alcohol – it's an odd feeling.

It
puts you beside yourself; into a place and position
that someone like *me*
    should be thoroughly used to, but it
  wasn't as surreal as so many of the times
  before. It was as concrete
    granite as a gravestone.
I'm not going to sit here and say
to you, that "I've *learned.*
my.
lesson," because
let's be
honest…
that's cliché and almost insulting,
given the amount of times I've had alcohol
poisoning,
driven drunk,
been jailed,
overdosed before and just all around almost killed
myself and
everyone around me. But this is definitely
    in the books…
I've taken a note,
  and it won't be forgotten.

Lacerate:

The worst is when they ask about your scars.
You don't know what to say, so you
just say you've had them.
"I've had them so long, I nearly forgot they
were there," …until you.

…

It's not the warmth of summer that reminds me to
breathe.
It's not the echoing light emitting from
brilliantly green grass, or the buzzing
of aerodynamic insects between flourishing
branches
of brushes and trees.

It's the smell. The *smell* reminds me to take my
next breath.

Please, if there's something above me, speed up this
process.
Wind the hands forward, with shots and cocaine.
Force me to remember the rhythmic periods,
looping
inter-dimensionally in my own reality,
with cigarettes and heart beats.

Please, let me forget to ask any further.

It doesn't exist.

Let me live.

It doesn't exist.

Lucidity:

Come on,
I've seen you do better –
I've thrown you though worse.
This isn't a drill…
Get up,
wipe your shins; stop
breathing the pill.
We gleam we've done better –
these thoughts aren't
the curse.
Get out your own way.

Get out of your own way.

… and write something that doesn't
 rhyme.

On Second Thought:

How long has it been, since
you had your own life
in your hands?

via morphine poison,
               or rippling blades
                   against your baby soft, blank wrist…

peering down some murky contour; a drain,
a barrel, a cell and its shadows… a River of Styx.

        peering into the wall of our
existence, like an ugly moth,
drawn to our orgasmic flames.

When was the last time you *knew*, for certainty,
that all of this was *real*?

Is there a now? can you feel it?
The envelope pressed against your soul…
Can you sense it
by passing by?
… and then,
                the decision is yours;

Spectrum:

See the love inside my eye.
Graze my lashes,
        pet my head –
                whisper "it's alright."
Kiss my ears with soft intention,
        grant me *ALL* of your attention,
melt into me
                this collision.
-*I* love *you*-
        Romance me
                this divine intimacy.
Slide your nails along my side,
digging... digging deeper,
                increase your stride;
run the razor,
        tighten the ties –
make me blind, make me abide.
See the dead inside my eye;
        Choke me 'till I cum or die.

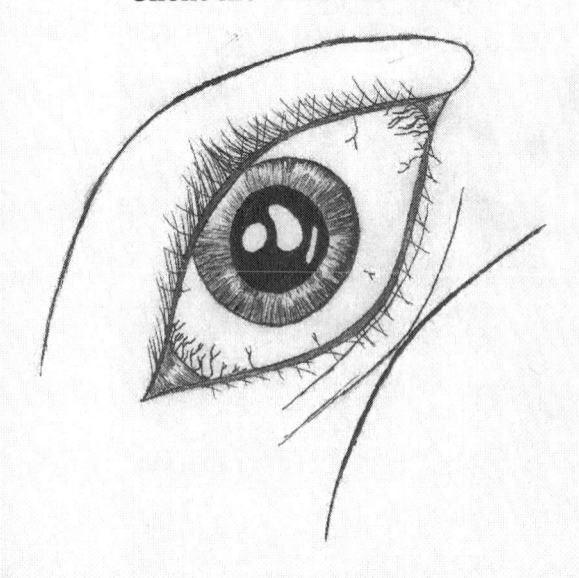

Poison Pouring:

You say that you'll go even though you know
it'll be shitty.
.
The smiles they'll show while
they hide all their pity in
half assed
almost witty distractions;
they know that if they
say your name enough
they'll get *some kind* of reaction…
but it's just not happening.
And you're alone
once more,
behind a vomit stained pale white door
with a rusty sink and
blinking black light.
You tussle in your mind about whether it
would be right, or *right*
 while your hands already
reaching for the bag.
You take this last drag
of your cigarette, making sure your cure never
leaves your sight;
you don't get a chance like this to embarrass
yourself
every night so you say "hey, I guess I might
as well.
It's not the future I'm worried for,
it's the past that's hell –

I'm try'na not remember;
to sooth the ever-growing ember in my mind.
So, I'll move this powder to a pretty limber

line, and - *snort*"

now look it – you're sick!
I'm not kidding, you can't stop wheezing, and your nose is *bleeding*!
This isn't funny, **stop laughing**!!
I'm worried for you man…
I'm worried about what's happening to my friend –
You're not you and it's like you barely know
me either –
I'm telling you dude, you *have* to let this end.

You're becoming the monster you swore
to me you'd never be, and after all the
family
and friends you pushed away, I'm the
only one left trapped to have to see
while you
crumble and brawl with yourself as you
stumble and crawl to the shelf to pour out
another line.
You're a walking bomb and you're ticking out of time;
every thought and breath becomes another crime
and it isn't just fine,
you're no longer mine **anymore**!
You're the scum of the earth,
remnants of the trashy man-whore who raised
you and your kin;

so, I'll look
in the mirror,
and I'll say it again…
"God dammit man, you need to let this end."

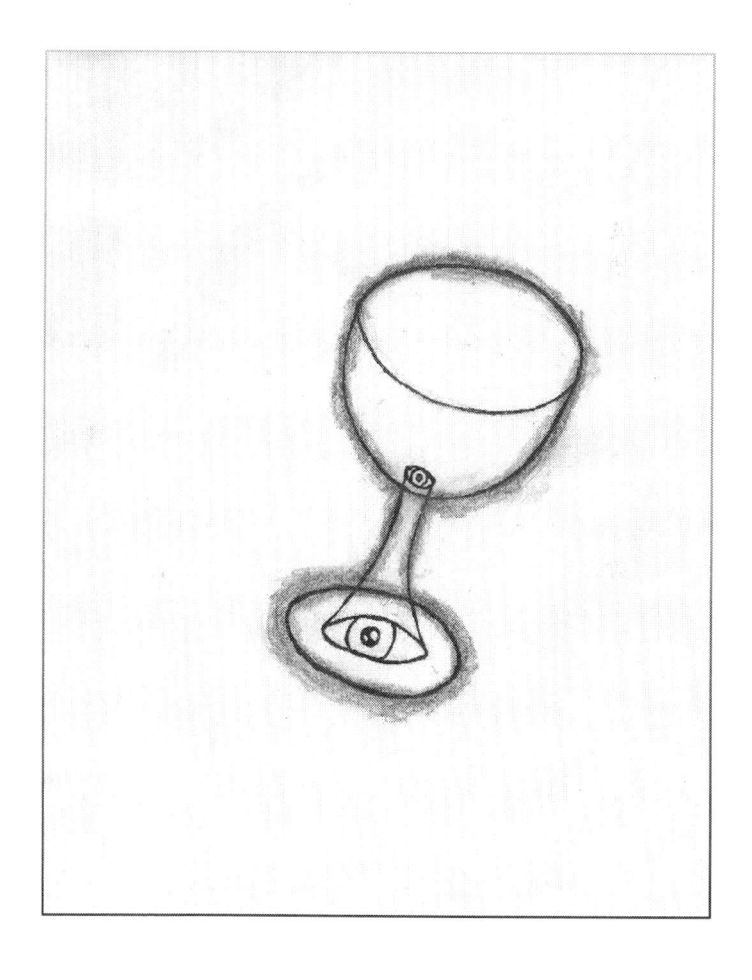

3
Neurosis

Normal Vain:

Dare to dream; to awaken the reconstructed
 hallucination,
  the hologram and all that's left to talk about.
Do you dare to stir the universe itself?
   the void and all its slumbered
glory...
Dare I say you may awaken the way your mind
consumes the world, like a spider causes chaos for
the gnat;
  like the nightmare of mosquitos is what's
natural for the bat.
  Dare I dare you to be deemed insane,
   to leave none left to decree
    insanity?

Gravity:

"There's no way out"
etched on the inside of my skull.
"I won't let you leave," it says
in echoes, down the hall.
Emotions always drooling, dumb
and dormant; oh, cruel me. Fun.
If I ever end this torment
then all of you will cry.
I shed a tear for every single day I didn't die,
and smile all the same.
Broke by an impulsive heart, and trapped
inside my brain.
"I hate you" "Kill it" "Divide their faith"
"Leave nothing in the wrong."
They pick and choose my type of space
and speak to me in psalms.
I'm convinced that I've been probed, but
I know that defines crazy.
A wire lodged within my lobe, recording thoughts
born rather hazy.
My sights, downloaded
by of those who sought to see
the life birthed by a baby.
Hell… maybe I am right…
Of course, maybe is a daisy; a seeded
thought that grows its stems in
hidden Fibonacci –
solidifying my delusion that aliens are
watching.
"There's no way out" I cannot share
the discomfort in my eyes.

Every time I've tried they've been
rejected as white lies.
I see one end;
in hope my mind will transit.
Rearrange my "D.E.S.P.E.R.A.T.I.O.N" and
see for me that "A. R.O.P.E. E.N.D.S. I.T."

Daem-eons:

So, let's think up confections of social "hoo ha's"
and contradictions… lets flex on these
decisions,
and rustle our decision-making muscle
for that word we've had to tussle with to
rhyme with things like "abortion"
"marriage"
"war" or the "ocean"
while,
simultaneously attempting to ingeniously
avoid drawn out sentence contortions….
and failing.

Let's pretend that deep down we don't
see what's really happened.
That it's been locked away into us;
our deepest, darkest repression.
How many nights
of eyes wide open
did this Earth curse us?
Is it so taboo to bring up truths
and points, like this?

Have you always run with the underdogs…?
The ones who are outcasts, and just don't fit well
with the rest.
The ones who say "cool kids"
with a negative connotation, and "normal"
like it's a disease they hope to never catch.
I've always found them to be what I had
most. In common with.

Just different enough for me, but, never like me.
I don't fit well with anybody,
really,
and it's futile that I've ever tried all this time.
…. What really is a demon?

Delicious, hypnotic, deluded, hybrid eyes
cease the long sighs of rising kings' harlot dreams,
and velvet lies.
Fluent is its quiet walk, which sings louder
than any whispered talk it could gawk into
your ear.
Lust as red as wine and roses, spiked with pain;
it drains the sane right from your fears.
Before it's clear your tear will sheer a salty
wound down to your chin. His breath will near,
your eyes, he'll mirror, and you'll disappear to join
his
kin.

If heart is home, but no heavens bloomed;
if hell has shown, and only gloom,
steer towards that hybrid demon.
If abomination is just as much
as your creations,
and lacerations are just vacations,
steer towards that hybrid demon.
If what's sane is deranged,
but pain is no gain,
and rain won't drain the weakened,
it's pure, the cure
casts by you here;
steer. Steer towards

that hybrid Daemon.

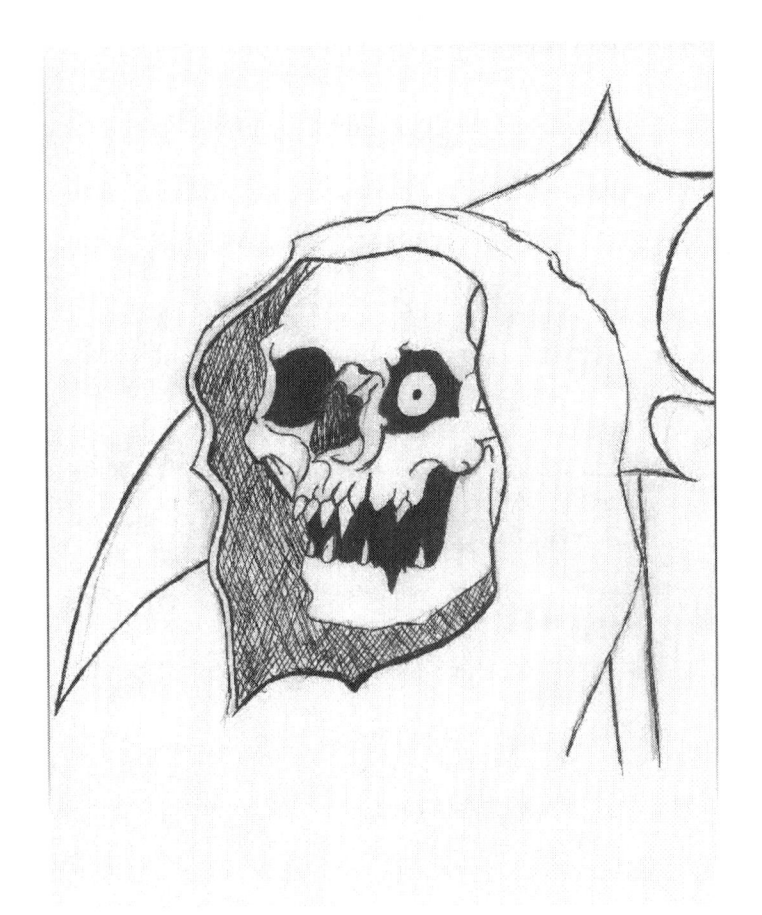

The race:

I am one of who I am.
Of breath that burns,
and faces turned in different lands.
The end is near from racing years
that we have ran.
        An end is near-
We pay for life, so death is free.
A world where names are sold
and faces bleed
society.
Like draining coins from a well,
like draining hope from misery.
Like bleeding God out of a demon,

like draining words from me.

Maybe I do it to make you feel,
to *relate*, to say **you're not alone.**
Maybe I do it to prove you wrong,
to knock your words
and build my own.

Maybe I do it to distract myself from the terror
of my senseless existence I've found
trapped within the mind I've grown.
I don't know, I can't remember…

I am one of what I am,
until you grow tired of me.
A panoramic turning wheel -
camera roll, tuning in and out of

reality.
A heartbeat of filter frames
with different knowledge and
identities.
Riding the spiral of what life seems,
locked by multiple chains of what I've seen,
recorded on parallel streams of duplicate, parallel
memories.
And no control of its direction.
Cut out for a path carved into eclectic sections.
Bound to this ride by its own interaction,
and by you, where each soul
is effected by every connection,
whether insignificant or true.

You are one of what I am.
Light reflects off of into each of us,
Connected by air
-shared-
brain waves,
ear strokes hearing vibrations off our throats
cusp, what we dare to say.
Reacting from so many actions
we lose track of their attractions or if we cared; they
collapse forever into who or where
we lose them -
Our intentions become a piece of who they are.

We are one of what we are,
the life span of a breath;
we don't see much very far,
or know the end of death.
Do we echo like a star,

or is what we have what's left?
If we never end, we were never born.
Are our souls really here for our flesh to be worn?
Do they hurt just as much
when our hearts have been torn?
Or are they interwoven
in this life we've been scorned.
Is "my" soul a masochist, if even there *at all*,
A collective deity of madness?
Will that ever end, in this torment of existence?
Or reincarnate as this space-time indifference;
the universe itself.

We are one
of nothing.

Talking in circles:

Coherent enough to spin on a spiral
to witness the cycle
and bring us full circle –
I'm conscious enough to be afraid
to live a lie;
to see the frayed edges our
time does tie.
This mysterious dimension of apprehension,
nightmare, and indifferent intention,
causes the side mirrors of
self-similar repetition,
and I alone cease to be.
Perhaps along with everything else…
Maybe… maybe…
But God, what do I know?
Evidence is arbitrary,
I'm just a kid, a ghost;
I'm no visionary – but
a host of panoramic data, and poetry.

Hand of God:

In the ever after, it rains
without wet
upon diamonds of flesh;

in the ends,
babes not yet
of breath
sleep soundly in their light.
They dream,
dream of falling judgement
upon first life.

We've all seen
    GOD
upon our entrance to
this mesh,
and we'll see
    IT
again, as we approach
sweet subtle death.

Earth is an Island in time:

A variance of hiccups, and toys left behind.
An insect, painting myself… painting myself
a way out of this mind.
Minds; dedicated to rippling
fire
that tastes of miracle.
Our slave ship, Earth, groans along alone
on its wire,
and you – you reek of charcoal
emotions, and sawed off shot guns;
broken potions and
spoken motions
laugh the laps we run…
n' round' n' round'
my words are
wet
with stars and suns.
The blood has spun
to pulsate slate blue
and silver radiance
atop their pendulum
of strings and webs.
Like Christmas lights,
or sugar, hexed;
we strain to drain
a model from our heads –
and paint ourselves, painting ourselves,
an infinity till' we're dead.

Of pasts in diamond crushed sand,
dirt, and grassy lands,

to harvest what whim of will;
the silhouettes stand
in stone, so still.
Ghosts of childhood,
genes, dreams,
and personhood we left
so far,
far
behind.
A temperament of being;
just being, and blind.
A void rendered constant unsure,
in thoughts, in wires, in eyes, in mind.

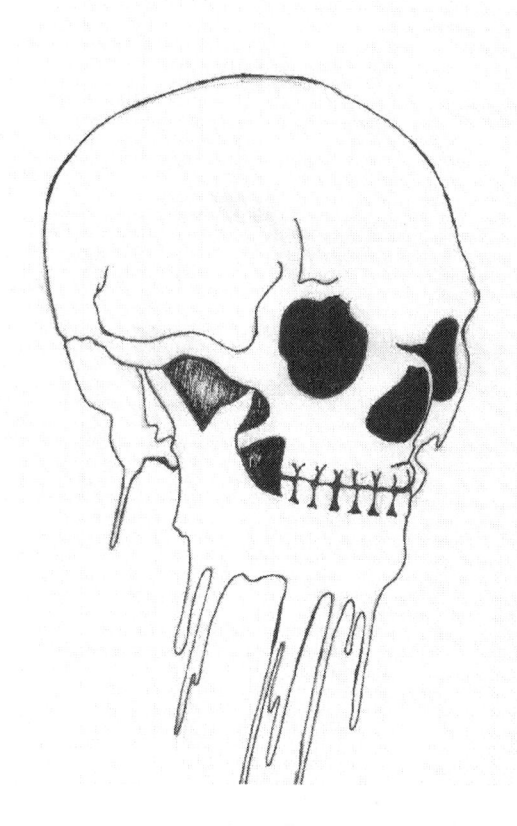

Ice age coming:

I'm several different versions of myself
spindling around in broken glass,
and every day
it gets worse.

They
call it a snowball
disease.
Then here I've been…

anticipating an
Avalanche;

I'm no different than
boiling water.

Tree of Life:

An autumn transition
of shallow Octobers; a rhythmic
emission of ends,
beginning over,
        and over…
this reflection of pupils,
        and clouds, and clovers –
the scrupled confection by
        our natures bright drover,
that is *will* begin, once over and over;
this beginning and end,
        this chaos and order.
This *holiest*
              of sins, on the skin
        of October –
                  an echo within
the life, and the boarder,
        of all that has been,
    and all that will be;
it all resides in
    the life of one
        dying tree.

Tuning in:

Diluted vision intoxicates the division of our tensor here.
A collision of infinity and our fourth wall skin;
a corpus-callosum of dimensions,
disregarded nonchalantly as
hallucination.
It's our dedication to our regular relations
with reality, which fuels the confusion that
anything more is merely
paranoid delusion.
A
mirror within mirrors,
an amplitude of my receivers' region;
dreams of nightmares in eyes of legions.
I will tithe your torment of judgement to my ever fleeting
moment, locked in space and time,
and with the rest I'll leave it far beyond the places left behind.

Deity:

And in these skies, expanding eyes,
that of these lies
immortalize,
"anything is everything,
 and everything is meant to die."
These
deity and dogma;
we live their lies,
 they eat our lives,
the names of those baffling hearts, enchanting
brains, and breaking time say, "everything
is anything, and energy, and repressed
cry - formed art,"
the shadows of our history,
collected in unconscious mind,
serving the basic firing of symbol – signal formed
reality,
from boredoms brutal casualty.
The thought formed DNA of
progressive thanatology.
Roman eagle, Atlantis myth;
anthropomorphized company
and reoccurring pith
of parables…
Born of a virgin, born of a miracle birth,
visited by the wise, the holy royalty,
enlightened and resurrected, the twelve,
the three,
the six, two,

the seven-eleven owned
by Hindu or Jew – it's all the same…
Let the sun stand still as you read these words:
The water you drink is only wine within your mind,
for in your mind resides the heaven… even then
it is nothing more
than a pitch.

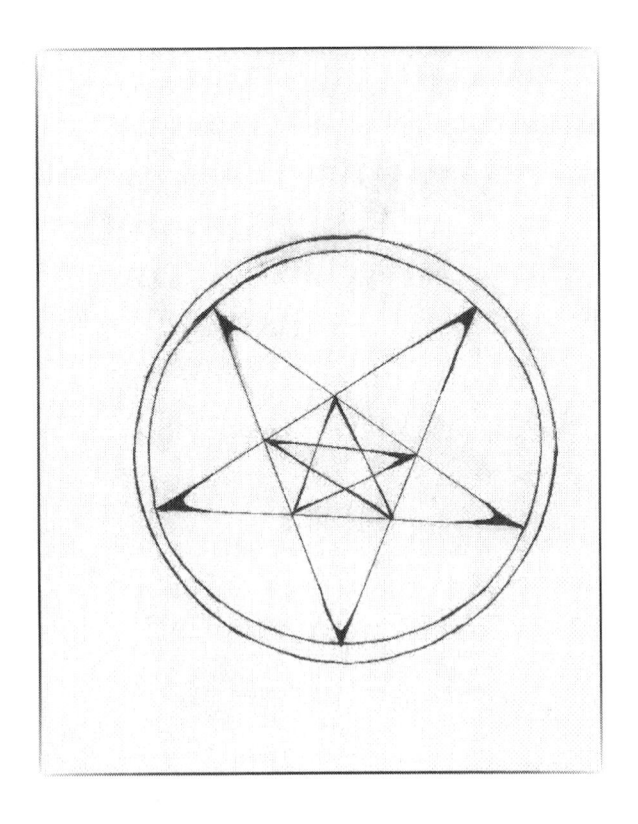

Cotard:

Don't let me distract you.
    Even the most withered commotion
doesn't warrant attention bliss.
    I've always believed in a
        kind of
           heaven, but there's doubt
in a heart like this; threadbare and stunted,
    in a line on the shore between being
caught hunted, and what comes then afore.
I swear it was just yesterday that I was alive…

    Now I feel smaller than air.
I don't know what happened… maybe I didn't eat
enough. My father always did say I should eat
more. I didn't know,
and after a while
I just didn't care.
    I just wondered when the worms would
begin their borrow through my hair.
    I wondered where they'd taken my …
well I would say "body," but that isn't fair.
Where did they take my amputee…
My corpuscle…
    My "used to be," because what ever
I am now, it surely isn't me.
Floating
    floating, between air.

The Experience of Butterflies:

It happens
and before anyone can tell you
why, or what,
it's collapsed into nostalgia.
Right through your fingers,
in the blink of an eye;
a perpetual conception
of a life, of a lie,
eighty milliseconds behind.
It's not the length of the line,
or the cut,
it's the depth which satisfies –
it's not the journey
which calls;
it's the experience of butterflies.
Captivating caterpillars in the form
of dying arts, ideas, drugs and hearts
crawling softly within our withering
minds,
eating every moment
out of courtesy of their code,
taking in the shades
of lives born colorblind
and transmuting our world
into the fragile wings
of butterflies.

Now?:

What is a clock without a tick
to suck out the life, life's struck
out of it?
What drains imagination if the batteries
if a toy runs dry?
Is it even possible to find...?
What. Is. Pain.
When skin becomes a violin?!
Where every stroke of the blade
releases an orchestra of
calligraphic sin.
Where every piece of my soul
becomes the ink
to this pen.
I live
everyday
to watch   myself die;
and sell every breath to maintain a thin sky
and
why?
What places could I go, if
I didn't know
my life was an object?

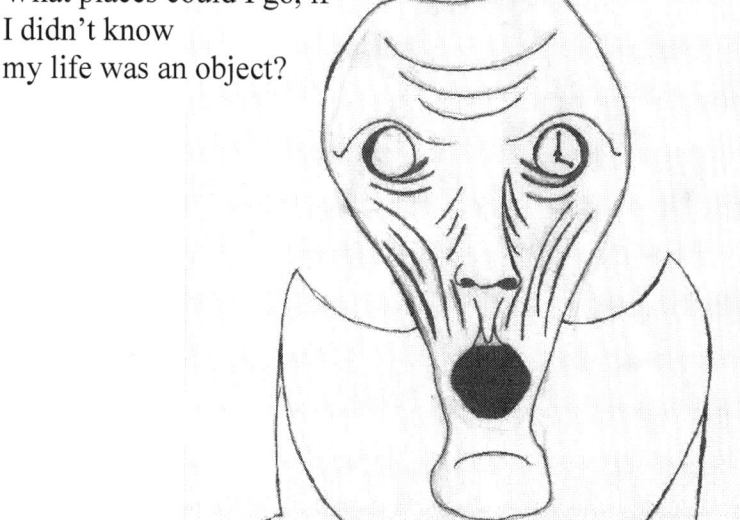

Droid:

I died this morning…
…and felt so oddly human today.
Leaving was always the plan, I guess…
Since our collision began, we address this ever changing
day.
This one day. On repeat.
While we sit with
restrained wrists and feet
to peer into our fractal void;
like rain travels through a mist, or a breath emits while my
driver's side door is hit by a public transit
and I'm wisped into a world of noise –
droned bones annoyed,
and crushed into oblivion.
This interaction was never meant for time,
but instead (perhaps) built to remind us
that we are so
oddly human.

Bloody screaming car crash:

I wish I could tell you that it's okay to come in…
                That the waters just
right
and the warmth of life's light will
melody its gift of
red spring,
summer flings,
and golden rings
into our night,
this night,
but this night I can only look back
                in horror
after the shock
and tidal splash with "don't."
do not get in to the water.
Don't even trickle its golden hymns across your toes.
Don't pay it a whim
so
that in the end you could know,
as a child surely knows
that in the end we'll truly be just
right.

Quantum Script:

If thoughts are air,
whether polluted or pure,
the lungs are iron, and
interacting as linked
pieces to the grand machine.
If thoughts are air,
and eyes are fair, our
hairs are watered
with the sensations of
now. The twine of time, laced around
our follicles would decorate
every fiber of our lobes with
exactly what it is. Maybe it does?
and that's why we feel so little.
To care to see no passage. Blind
and bound by our addiction
to purpose.
To bear no swollen message, kind of
found amongst the rotted
messiah carcass.
Then coughing phlegm
of bullshit reason to which
we worship
and bow;
Never asking why, only
"how?"

The Blender:

Climb up what you pull down…
from a dream of draining water
swirled around and grounded
by the static in the breath which you
hold.
It's a shock to our shells
that tells us we're alive, and
it's lies from our lovers
that makes the truth so
                bold.
Tears fuel the sheers that cut down bad fruit,
which molded on golden trees, christened
to us by drooling brutes;
An Anthropocene of relation.
Fears clean the mirrors worn as masks by our
friends,
who witnessed our souls as they
discovered their ends.
Push and then pull
         what you climb up to
              fall down,
as the water from the drain,
drains tears to the ground…
to be soaked up by clouds and
released in a dream;
screaming a tapping beat against the creases
in the street.
Push to the ends of all of reality, and pull
back for our eyes to see,
and minds to truly understand
and know,

what it means to fully be,
a yes and a no.

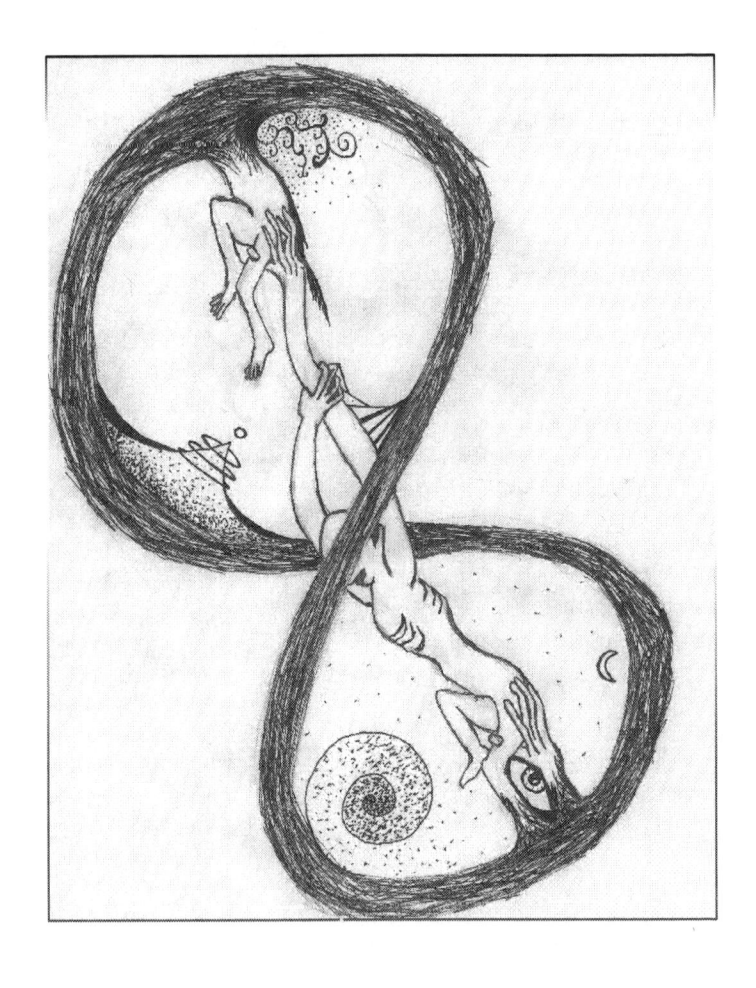

Basement Dumb Bell:

timid little critter of the basement
biosphere,
too cautious to make a sound…
    what if it is heard?
Better to stay small, and docile,
    out of sight amongst
the black mold and rotted
falling ceiling tile.
The basement is its personal mars,
    a convenient little planet
buried deep away from the
cruel judgement of
the mainlanders, who are far too
old and foreign to
compliment its extraterrestrial traditions.
Better
to stay below the radars of
these symbiotic
android apes,
of whom would chew
apart its confidence.
What if they come close?
Though they're far outside,
what if?
What if?
It just wants to be comfortable
in its slighted
damp corner.
Leave it alone, please,
Don't knock, just go about your own business
And let it grow alone.

Something or nothing:

Is it better to be?

There are characters who will never know your name….
There's a game
        of blame,
                and shame,
that pains the domain our brain remains.
There are gods of fame,
criminals insane,
      animals deranged,
           and I crawl within this bane
that everything is
meant
                        to flow in this waning
                leaning way….
      And that it's alright,
it'll be okay to have a thing
        rather than no thing
           in this planetary stay.
Because I know deep
down,
            the way that I stay sane…
is there are people out there who will never know my name.

Boredom'd:

Exciting new times are here, brand new things to see.
New games and gadgets,
toys and drugs,
but you'll always run out,

eventually.
Run

around mad, and confused. Aimlessly,
begging to be given to
the scraps that feed the slimy,
black worm that's starving
your art,
chewing on the base of your spine,
nesting at the center of your heart.
It chokes your adrenal glands
and drinks serotonin,
digesting your happiness to shit it out in one motion.
It's the apocalypse; the unveiling of illusions,
that which has raped us and forced us to swallow.
It is the cardinal sin; punishable with death, by being fed to cannibals.
At least *they* have found creativity in their illness, existence.
It is the motivator of the flesh,
to wear a thin dress,
and beg all night long to be freed from its clutches.
The extinction of love…
Tortured death of the soul.

Gourmet:

I can see through you here,
you tasteless crèche of
recoiled madness, sheered solemn and
veered by the taste of flesh.
What smoke, what solitude,
of muscle skin…
What birthing appetite, this natural sin
of man and child and cockroach –
the gums do bend to bleed wine like sap
of Calla Lilies and pubescent wires
wrapped around your knives and teeth.
Of rawness oozed on hands of hands,
and blood on pale paper covering blood,
housing the lunacy of this murdering hunter
and perverted hunger; the man.
The wild animal, an apex predator so collectively
starved of any fulfillment. The man that
eats man, forever in an endless
and insatiable growing rotted pit.
The killer who kills like his life depends on it.
Never to waste, like a thoughtful idea, any part
of its food; any cartilage or tendon, or the bio-
solution drip of the eye, staring into its pulverizing
coffin of teeth tongue buds. An intestine rope
designed to be broiled,
burnt or boiled; marinated
in marrow and oregano thyme.
My wish,
is the wish of all cannibal minds;
to be caught
red handed

in a clean yet tainted breath
of the loved one devoured amongst
lovers.
To be strung up or shot
in a fit of irony; only the kind
of theater truth to never fully
be discovered… oh,
        how her heart reeked
of design… how her hair
glared brilliance before
it shriveled up into fire, like a closing
rose upon the night. Why,
I'd never dare impersonate such
lullabies of potent pity and shock. A mother made
new and beautiful on china, glimmering
as salmon and cod do among candle light. A mother
deserving of the most animated grave, after such of
her criminal son betrayed her; the epiphany of being
the rock to his rock has slayed her, and now she's
delicious once again. A final feeding
from a maddening doe; her tit offered a racing
lamb a beat of slow, and calm, as he chewed
his victim one after another.
He can never forgive the drive within him,
and he will never forget
his lovers.

It isn't always void:

Deep pillars swallow white echoes.
They find no point in talking
if you take it so serious,
instead of letting go to what's naturally delirious.

Singing *Goddesses* suit this sleeping *goat*.
Tickling glass stained night trenches so

open new windows
with haste…
Empty your rays

Sleep…*Shhh*,

listen to my whisper,
scratch through the density of night.
Follow my breath into your ear.
Allow me to awaken sight.
Allow me to fill your soul with fright,
so that you may use it to your advantage.

Release your ***might*** to bring my delight,
in causing this structure damage.

Steer clear from the blood, and all its vintage,
or it may drink you whole.
Its droplets drip in acidic carnage,
and dim your light till dull.

Or merge your ego, transcend with me,
drink with me

and eat
what's left.

Brows:

Sweet candy I beg you
turn your gaze,
for I am unattired.
Cold cornered and godly given cards
as white as
Nebraskan winter hilariously
glares its poker face
back through my mirror.
Please, please dear, don't look at me.
I'm so unclean without

my everyday mask
of mashed lipstick and pearly blush.
Oh queen I've been hunting, I'm hounded by your
absence again.
        And how I wish this made sense,
                this world without heels, or fur,
or foundation. I wish
I was content and beautiful without

        a veil of chemicals and Shea Butter.
I just don't feel that way.
Instead I'm a canary imprisoned in a seagull.
Instead I'm a diamond vase
        accompanied by a rotting corpse in
the Aztec tombs of Tenochtitlán. I'm a doll in a
                sweater of suede,
a dress of peacock and polyester,
                    and I beg to be anything but
plastic… to feel anything but shame
without my meta-mask.

Charlotte Rose:

"Nothing matters, and we know nothing matters, and that matters."
"There ain't nothing nowhere and it's getting to be less than nothing, all the time… nothing is worth it."

Ask why we're here,
I dare,
to strive for what may bring more of what we've had all along.

Cut deep into dark corners of a sphere;
there is no satisfaction here,
no end to our chase
in chaos,
in our infinite multiverse,
and we become nothing short of a black hole,
spinning, spinning…

delicate dictations of our pedals spiral us into our wine drenched core,
and out again to search for more.
Forget that rose of truth,
the realm of real, and go back to sleep;
forget to forget the question, "why are we here?"
    remember instead, please, to ask in
confidence why it is we know we're sleeping.
Ask,
jerk awake,
fly away, and ask…
"why do I know how to ask who I am?"

Pale Sand, Cold Hands:

Dreams with blood so real, I can taste it
        upon my lower lip.
I can sludge it within my hands
        in a desperate attempt
to stop   the drench.

        push, pat, and frantically exhale –
did I shoot you?
No, there's no way one mistake could deliver
so. much. Damage….
        Please, please tell me I didn't do this!
Oh, how now I miss the winter; how I wish
This fog would lift us clean
and clouds hold still as the
moonlight passes by.

I can't say I'm innocent, not
unless
you morph back into my dearest doe. Not
unless
you show me which antler branch
impaled you – which bind of love coerced you
to take such leap of faith?
Let me lend my nails and teeth
to mend your punctured ribs. I'm in the end with
you; for every piece of me you ask then any piece
I'll give.
Now that I'm force fed your nightmare, my vomit
crucifies our significance; for in the end I was
always meant to lie. For us, my doe, for we were
always meant to die.

Cubical:

Terror tears through the marrow of tomorrow;
the skeleton of brittle unsure.
What of... What of the groans
behind the bones of my smile?
What of my dear, my sanity?
Will I ever have the strength
to run these mental miles?
Do I dream beneath your clarity...
It's the insecurity enduring me that panic lungs deflate.
That pink hearts beat race,
bones turn to twist and break
on this winding road of a twisted life I hate
and know.
It's never old, but always late.
I'm always cold and iced innate
and barely bold enough to sell the poison sold to me in fate.
Fate?
...I guess monsters do hold names.
Shit.
        Breathe.
                Now.
It's robbed again of me,
this demon in my mouth strapped in a symbiotic feed.
Biomechanic fire clutch...
Dilute in tragedy this angels lust
to suffocate.
Faith? Who knew toxins could wear names?
Will I ever hold a job...?

Will I really keep this love –
Will I ever find a god?!
Aside from violence, Desert intensity,
and pain?

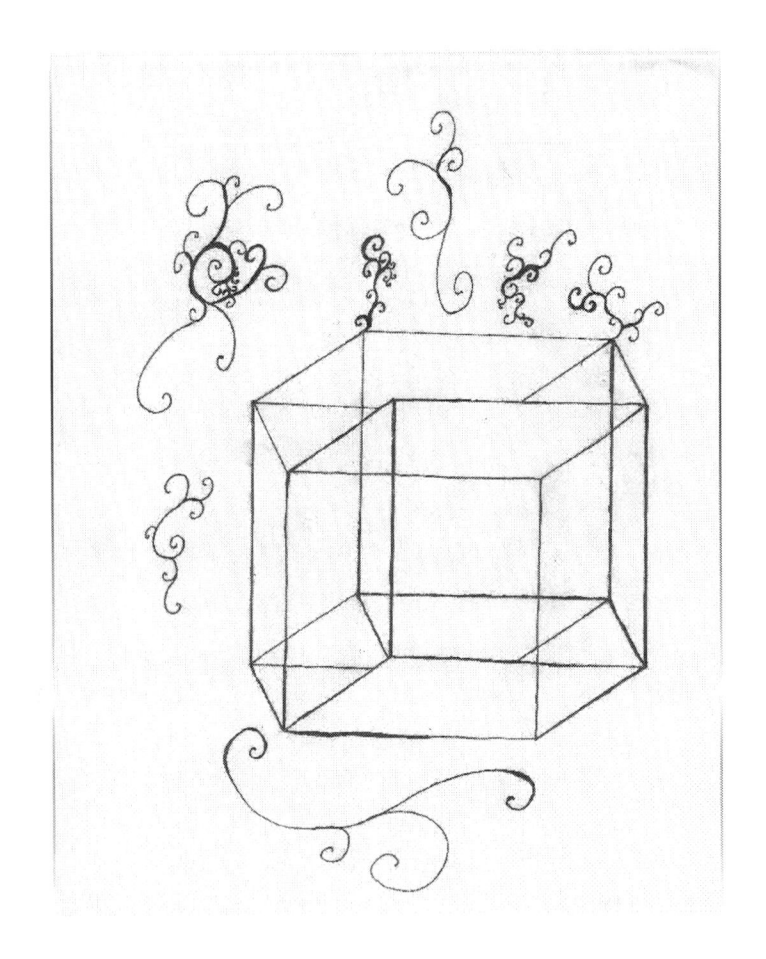

Reflection:

She said, "you're tortured,"
"you've got some…"

And that,
I'm crazy.

I'm crazy in my…
suit and tie,
my luscious lie… she said,
"you kind of want to die."
And
in a couple of years,
I'll make about a teacher's salary,
but I'm well on my way "to an overdose or prison,"
"He's never going anywhere – "
TO owning my own company…
It's not that farfetched **TO**
"assume you'll have the money"
for freedom and happiness.
"Always the craziest ideas."

"some of my best memories are
            with you."
                I
never have to die, no matter
how much I want to.

Attention Deficit Disorder:

Faces melting in the dead of night
unto the pupils of calculation.
Hands come lose right before
your eyes,
to demonstrate their dedication.
The moon howls down its sober light
as it pulses medication
for the space and time you breathe in,
in transcendent hesitation.
Grassy lawns like water beds swim
shadow pawns around my head and
I haven't heard a word you've said;
I've been holding hands with dead
as they pull me towards a thousand
different
places.

Where You've Been:

Creatures are rising to mind, feeding
on the questions to any answer I
offer.
Flies made of soot disguise the
creature eyes of my imposter.
There's no hiding from the perceived,
just a yearn to turn away. Creatures
rampant now relieve the recessions of my
brain, and dance in blooms across
the ceiling slant and plane. Gods reflection
of the grave swirl in black and shades of
powder to the rhythm of my breath,
until the rhythm, they take hold of.
Prayers crawl in this moment
to and fro
above my teeth, within my gums –
within the blood inside my lungs,
hosting every kind of worm and bug
your hell could fathom.
This life makes no sense, and of this
senselessness I dream in real time
to reconstruct a world
that's dense, a moment real,
a life that's mine.
Until I see the creatures stuffed of questions,
starved of answers, and reconstruct
to remember it wasn't ever…
It wasn't ever mine.

The Human Animal:

A twitch of my little finger.
Brain, recognizing brain.
What is it reaching for?
A firing nerve lingers in flesh,
like smelling rain and death –
is it insane to guess that
I'm not me at my core?
I chew me up like an apple…
Every thought to dissect and
       chew through myself,
and digging deeper I grapple
to know just
what it is that I'm reaching for.
If my brain is its own being, attentive
thoughts spewed spot light
like
television fuzz,
organized to order, then I can't
trust that what I'm seeing isn't merely a
boarder or frame of the painting
it won't allow me to feel.
If my brain is its own, then am I
even real?

In This Suicidal Art:

Well sullen words burn,
                left behind while
I shiver, while I
speak my mind;
why
      can't you
                forgive?
Sulk and milk your teenage coil;
don't spring your step,
just melt
and boil.
I'm rusting like a shiv.

They say you've got to feel
        you've won,
but we tick the same –
the same we run;
these moral bullets from
a cunning gun
spell hell;
that I've little left to live.
When all I ever wanted
                Was to hold me down.
I'm the darkest mistake,
        tickling the wake of
Mercury's crown. The
war of more, fought and adored
on Venus ground.
July   is over,
    Autumn is falling;
I beg orange clovers,

for luck, I'm calling,
        that maybe I can turn this dream
around.
Lucid orange clovers
falling,
falling to the sound
of a completed
past.
It's the merciless thoughts, fought
like mercenaries against me,
which mistakes this pain to last.
The vision of a loaded
weapon, full of blood
and confetti color.
The vision; a monumental collision
of my condition
with what's tangibly cool
dolor. Pull softly
my trigger
to rip out all of me with sheer force;
untangling each memory with explosions
in each cells divorce;
I've blown my mind apart.

Call Home:

Present positioned in conjunction of history.
Of a pond of time with droplets of Giovanni's
misery.
The calculation of empires,
hued and dunned,
like an infrared Rome, or Egypt tomb.
In the now, even Earth's Rome has fallen.
Ages of empires, abandoned,
forgotten.
propelled through extinction, a vile
genetic code, injected
in maggots and teeth and apes.
The final stretch of survival –
our selfish DNA.
There is no source of our
Life, beyond that.

Subjective Morality:

Authentic to what?
Sincere to an election of faces
one face fakes to be?
Mirroring masks deemed healthy by
society?
Where's the landing strip
for this flight of authenticity?
How clean is the departure…?
A personality pure of intent,
deemed self-centered –
the possibility of altruism by philosophy
is hindered.
The cataclysm tapestry of assimilated
interaction endures, in this simulated
grudge fueled merry-go-round
hearse.
How do you know who they think they are
is who you think they are?
How could they know you?
Do you?
What gives you the *right* to *assume*
that who they are
and what they do, is *true*?
Doing nothing is where authenticity blooms,
and yet nothing
is
impossible to do.

Restless Goodnight:

Every day I'm losing my fucking head.
I'm starting to love
the songs of the dead.
See, even bleeding hearts run out of red.
I'm not afraid of the dark. The natural
state of the universe, is night.
My blood is black and shadows move
within the parameters of my sight.
Two left turns make a right but
God damned me a wrong turn
of life.
I'm angry, you're beautiful.
Could I lose my soul tonight?
It doesn't belong to me anyway.
I should fucking
kill
myself…
… maybe this weekend.
If I get around to it.

I Wish I Could Help:

I'm not identifying with the emotion quite well;

I feel numb. Muddled. Disconnected.

I still feel creative, like
I still have it in me to express myself thoroughly.
      but driving today...
           Watching the license plates and rear
      windshield reflections of our overcast fog...

I literally felt like I was sitting in my passenger seat
the whole ride home;
and now all my trail of thoughts are headed straight
off the cliff.

You're losing me man… What's in those woods?

Because I want to be wrong,
but those words have quite a riff –
I've heard this before.
I wish you could help too.
I put a world around this door,
my friend, this knocking's nothing new.

I'd forgive myself, if you could let me,
instead I'm left forgiving you –
it's okay, I'll be alright,
there's nothing to really worry about.
I'm just stuck in my own head,
I guess…

Air:

This poem is lengthy.
Like the long strides of the pillow tides
as you
roll yourself over and see
that it's a quarter past 2:00 pm
and you haven't brushed your teeth yet.
Where *so much* could've happened in the day
but it's a lifetime too late
and everything is taken up by the space
that you shouldn't inherit.
Where you've
made up your mind,
there's *no reason* to make your bed
when your *just*
gonna fall
back
asleep
in it anyway.
… this poem… is lengthy.
Like the **thoughts**
strung out
on prescription medications
and their own inhibitors.
They're victims of a genocide
between existence, and
happy.
Buried, feet first
hands bound
behind the pressure found
from tired eyelids and syllables
bent

to camouflage sadness.
…
Syllables like, "I'm okay,"
"I'm just tired,"
"It's a long day,"
see we're rewired to accept
the benefits of ignorance
in a face to face conversation with
depressed relatives.

Everyone's just playin'
'Frogger' with their thoughts,
dodging the misconception of a creative
imagination and
cancer,
where the only difference is social acceptance.
What if we really did die in 2012?
What if life is only lived
deep within our minds, and
their power,
which we don't fully understand –
is the same force that holds us down
when we're trying
so hard
to stand?
And if
our problems are merely self-inflicted by the brain –
as solutions awaiting their own presence?
A game… deviously casted out
as an attempt to counter act the boredom
of our own existence…
What if this is limbo?
How do you *know* that you're alive,

have you ever
really
tried
to die?

Thoughts – strung out on their own road
where every mile they've ever sowed
seems longer than
any time they've ever owned.
Thoughts like
"kill yourself to prove these theories…"
Thoughts like, "*these people*
are simply projections to
a subconscious reaction
to your inner demons."
Thoughts like, "*every effect*
has an equal and opposite reaction
according to Newtons third found equation…
so, if our universe never ends…
did it ever *really* begin?"
thoughts that *none* of this is real
and I'm *trapped* inside of a dream
made of
fifth dimensional beings and their
incomprehensible intelligence –
you're a 4-D *hologram print*
hanging on the bedroom wall
of a dead beat, mid-twenties
god.
These thoughts that scream
that I'm not in control
and the things
that control me

are without any hold of purpose,
or meaning.
Everyone just…
tying different flames to wicks,
hoping for another day to drearily
kick
rocks on top of our world
that *groans*
throughout this reflective void…

Or maybe it's just me…
and maybe accusing the rest of you
with this *cancer*
is one way to live with
this reality.
Maybe it's genetic and I'm
echoing an illness of distilled misery.
Maybe my time doesn't flicker
or blink
like the stars of your vitality,
but instead it's glowing
dimly like the grass underneath a
hectic moon.
I'm this nihilistic collector of gnosis
in the socket of my skull,
collecting his plastic mind
too soon to find the mindful kind like him…
if only for a moment to feel like
I've got a kin.
Not a body, nor a soul,
could realize we're
growing old
from the first time that

our hearse could verse our chariots.
It's the body, not the mind,
that I've *bottled* so deep inside and convinced myself
it doesn't exist…
but it… doesn't exist. Right?

Realistic pessimist in this epileptic paradigm
of masochistic relationships
with the sadistic eclipsed us,
and left us lonely and blind,
with chances slim to find that
homely divine of a time
well spent to fly and find ourselves.

I'm *running* towards death, because I can't
have bad health when "*bad*" is not a word
that exists in all of my minds wealth –
it's
cursed with fire.
The wires and chemical colliders inside of
this buyers' skull.
Fire that burns the feelings and thoughts,
stealing the sought ceiling that
any action I take, has any meaning at all.

… but then it feels like falling…
Falling like a tear drop tears through the air,
on to the cold palms of a dying grandmother
amidst her final, gasping breath…
the transparent silent *banshee*
of chemical emotion erupts
across a plane of indifferent elements

and oxygen
until it *crashes* out of existence.

Like all of you, I'll die in waves
of memories that fluctuate into a legacy,
and reverberate into yesterday.
Like all of you, I'll die
Like the sands of an hour glass,
we pass one another in a billion different ways,
metaphysically touching each spherical surfaces of our soul,
and forever escaping into the realm beyond
with everything that once made us feel
so at *home* with life.
Touch. Taste. Sound. It's all
temporary and bound by the chains
of our own mortality.
It's a heavy pill to swallow,
but every day we're forced to face
this reality, in one way or another –
like the death of a neighbor,
or the thoughts… of a delusional mother.
Thoughts like, "we're all born to die
as souls that lie awake, to lie and take
away everyone else's joy."
Thoughts like, "chemical reactions
by our schemas interpretation
of extrinsic stimuli are
overlords to us, and our
brains are just their toys."
Thoughts like
"a child that's devoid of fear,
will lead itself to its own death,"

and "your production to the hate machine,
is fueled with every breath."

I am the lie.

Biomechanically engineered by a
highly cognizant pioneer –
advanced and entrepreneuring
in multidimension information ideas.
It's *paradoxical* the relation to their
consciousness levitation and mine. Our
position is spacious, yet still, quantumly
connected through space and time –
I'm *racing* probabilities for the chance
that our pairings are merely
a dance
of cyclical lifelines.
It's me.
It's me, and you, and everything
that we've ever been through,
connected like an amorphic flesh design,
defining the prolific envelope of what's been,
what is,
and what could *only ever be*.
And when we get there,
you, with me,
I'll remember how these thoughts would *never*
escape me.
but then I'll see that I am these thoughts.
For these *thoughts*
are what make me.

4

love

Psychic:

I was in your eyes,
in the green of lake Bodom,
and when they glanced at a warm cloud
in autumn,
I combined our lips
   -
to be awoken by your spell
that wished to make my dreams
come true.

A moment caught twice,
by two
in a forced déjà vu;
a work of art I'll never be able
to make up to you.
Never.

Family:

I'll tell you
                just one fear
that's blessed itself
my head.

It's that,
       I won't make the one's
            held dear

                                      proud,
before they're dead.

The Tub Was Green:

Dusted light penetrates our window
Like lines of Morse Code
… --- …

the water that binds me remains warm and low.
The color of love is green.
Is this love?
                        Without love you can elude
      hate.
Our naked body seems to gleam
the incessant hunger, like always being
early, and always feeling late.

The tub was green, I was innocent,
his game was bait.
Memories made and put to slumber.
Forced and choked and burned like lumber;
this puppet that I am.
Pull my strings,
push me onto you
All these things that you went into;
my mind, my identity, my physical body.
      Lubrication is code for spit,
your member deep inside,
      and all I hope is my vomit
won't hasten up your stride.

Remember now, it's not a lie,
It's not a dream,
You're really there,
You really cried,

He really lied,
You really died.

Spring metal veins beneath a mattress skin
thin, worn, and torn to allow a clutch
to still. To safe.
In cotton and blood
to what they do as what's been done
by someone else.
As mud is felt;
mud is felt between white fabrics
overlapped and freshly cleaned –
white yarn ties in liquid streams to scream
and burn my throat that this
is just
a game.
It's just a game
it's just a game we shouldn't play
but we can't turn it off.
It's just a game that's gone insane
Inside this hell of cloth.
Too early to know protest…
Too late for fighting breath,
and split apart to recollect
this earliest of deaths.
Keep pushing to suck me dry,
Keep drilling to make me cry.
Muffled, tied, all mind spent like time
to win this endless game…
and though I'm shamed,
I still remember the blame.
Let you feel what I'm going through.
This will be over soon.

Gas Station Date:

Reds 100 in less than five minutes.
If I need to talk about anything, you're there
in six,
like a chain inhale
on knuckles so pale
where helping me
is an added fix.
So
I deliver a problem from
time to time
of every exhale betwixt,
and keep you around
because… I don't know why…
this nicotine melancholy
mix.

Blazer:

Do you dream about me too?
It's been over a year
and my brain *still* tries to talk to you;
Cutting salutations into its
virtually constructed simulation.
Sometimes it feels…
like it's a note within a bottle,
where at the bottom is the sip which
throws it full throttle – across dimensions,
stars,
and all the various planes of wherever you are…

I want to say I miss you. Maybe not the ***real*** you,
but
the you I *swear* I thought I knew. And…
I want to say I thank you, because,
at the time, you were
the only thing
that's real, and all I needed
was a simple truth.
…and now you're dead,
and I don't know what that means… but I beg
that you're at peace.
I beg that life seems as great
As you once seemed to be.
Goodnight.
-love,

MK:

You're an angel.

A stage:

Is this how you'd like me to pretend?
Pieces strung together
in ether, art, performance –
all at once are ripped apart again.
Compartmentalize what
is seen, what I show, selling out;
selling you the partial world
I own. A package half
buried and disassociated am I,
because
it's what you love;
god damn, it's what you love, and I love you.
A balancing act, acted like an underlying
script in everything I say and do.
How the hell am I to love, or better yet,
be loved,
if every concussion of desperation
is ruptured in isolation.
It is so. *Good*. To see you.

Cowards Tune:

Am I shaking?
Or are you
okay?
Reading thoughts-
Can I or can they?
Is this communion, or dissension?
With or against?
Thoughts are
slipping.
Can you just tell me the rest?
Completely blank-
Not much on my mind.
Flick.
Crack.
"Ignore that" but
I'm already blind.

With your nose against mine
and my eyes
in your eyes
Is it me?
"What's going on inside your mind?"
I can't answer that well…
I don't think I can tell
whether or not I have cracked;
if I even have a shell…
Maybe not.
Its abstract
or perhaps been attacked.
Now the thought is

slipping
and I'll never get it back,
That's a fact.
My thoughts cannot diffract
past this wall which blocks my consciousness
and keeps me so anonymous…

Your breath is growing ponderous
as you ponder this
wondrous wilderness
grown in tenderness and care,
likening the woods with which
into I stare,
to every coil, and strand, and lock of my hair.
As I am locked on your eyes,
my pupils dilate in size,
yet I am trying to demise this confusion;
Are these lies?
Are we no longer in disguise?
Here I am in a struggle with my mind
and your lips only keep me blind
in a stare.
I can't stand my own tongue
blocking the thoughts that are there.
Locking me silent within my own snare.
It's almost unfair that I cannot repair
The links that bound my words to your
ear.
But when I catch the gaze of your
Fear I melt into your love,
my dear,
settling peace between two doves
and come to rest in you, my mirror.

Your fear of thoughts you've done me wrong,
and I have sought,
at last,
at long,
to see that in your arms I shouldn't be;
but that just isn't how I feel.
For F.E.A.R. is merely
False Evidence Appearing Real.
see, I love my dove,
my Venus dune,
the gods above from which you tune.
We cycle through like earth and moon,
and soon we'll bloom like spring to June.
And every day after that,
that I'm with you.

I can't live without you.

Long Distance Reincarnation:

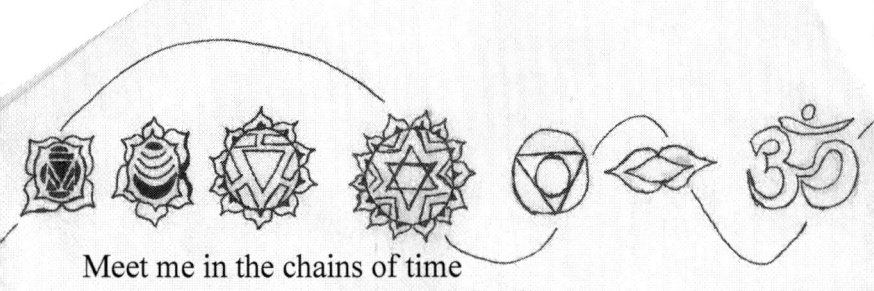

Meet me in the chains of time
where we've painted cursive clouds
and hearts are loud with echoed lime.
Fire trembles indigo eyes the bluest
songs of star lit skies.
To rewrite sin is our only crime;
to run full circle chanting chimes
that all that's wrong is really
fine.
That all that's wrong
is really fine.
Orange with yellow skin as red begins
we find our start on, off again, on again
as red begins this breath of violet calm
it boils in.
We take nothing
but ourselves into the white.
So, meet me betwixt the dark and light;
for there I'll find
My love and mirroring life.

Heroin:

The whole world is insane, and inside of you.
A collective untamed, collided view of
theology's moralities, and their ticking hands
of reality.
Kaleidoscopic dualities soon boil over,
revealing patterns snapping out of place from
disorder;
collapsing eternally to their original source.
Chaotic creations explode in divorce
from a star, from a beam, from a thought in a
dream…
So far and astounded does
the emptiness leave me; a chaotic creation
of an unknown location.
Wrapped to go deep within,
in a layer of skin, and a different vibration.
Discovering in awe my own damnation
to this planetary game.
Trapped to live my whole life,
in a whole world that's insane.

Blizzard on Ice:

Snores and fan blades stroke the 5:43
like whiskey,
wine,
and piano keys.
She's sound,
and floating within herself and my bed.
While I,
I slam down piano keys and another shot
to my head.

It smells like
    cigarettes,
        and cricket burns.
        It feels like tears,
    on false shames,
    and I follow her breath
with my hands 'till I turn, and realize,
how I barely know this queens
name.
but she's asleep in my room,
    my corridors,
my tomb,
        and I know the sun will
        rise again soon,
where maybe… maybe she'll
be my June.
        But, it's December.
        The fire's ember, and
    I'm out of my flame.
    I've lost respect for the others,
        I've lost the love

>   of the game.
> My heart can't hold yet another;
> we'd be so cold with each other,
> excluding how we fuck
> until
> >   our demons are slain.

Another sip, and it's on to the next.
Another day that which melts with the rest.
Another girl, another face,
another soul in this race of "just sex."

To you:

We miss the feeling of a smell
being more than a sensation of home.
What am I to do now?
Now that the essence of sound is freeing;
the taste of a rose unlocks a plethora
of visual uprisings;
crescendos of oddities
surround the blanket over my feet
fire, scream
"TALENT!"
Talent.
I don't *have* talent;
I have no gift of articulation.
I am nothing but an organizer of the ambiguous
for you to collect
some pieces
of a mirror.

...

There's a sacred place inside your eyes;
a beacon where your soul's light
shines,
like Kronos resides within your mind.
If I could turn back time,
I'd know
to love the lies… and sign more
blood in tides that stride
across our now colliding line;
who knows what could've been?
If I had only loved the lies,
who knows what could've been…
Contracts of souls built on

sweet nothings whispered slowly
by the dead,
contact our roses guilt beating on
our chest and
heating up our heads.
Every dew silhouetted on the pedals
of our bodies glisten red
with the venom of bad hobbies and
a story that we've bled.

We dance along the relation of a broken heart,
and I do my best
to capture each pulsation,
because with you beloved;
existence is art.

Expectations:

Anticipate nothing beyond what's clear
        to you, and
you might make the days that give you
hope, last
into the twilight.
These are animals,
these are gentlemen –
these are carcasses and we let them in.
This is her game,

and I'm trapped
playing it.
This is our name as we're saying it:

Romantic Misanthropes, juxtaposed to oblivion.
Juxtaposed on infinitude,
The void
Inside my words.

…

i shouldn't miss you.

A poets' analogue:

It's the foreign land of 4:00 AM,
and like a freighters siren howl,
it strikes me brave I've arrived within
this cycling cusp.
My Night, she rolls unto the beach of light,
as climactic as a gasp.
As conclusive as a sprouting lily,
as confident as dusk –
and I turn to retire,
but ask her, "please,
before i leave,
would you hold me like it was the last time?
Hold me in your deepest shade,
and mock my mind,
once more of final irony
to kick my dreams.
For this to be the last of me you see, it might;
my lushest supreme, my sweetest queen,
my gentle goodnight."

Co-dependence:

I think you are pornography;
stimulating my animal mind
with the best kind
of hate,
and I simply don't *want* to let you go
about your day
thinking
you're art.
I'm dulled by you,
so I'm pulled into a poisonous image,
untrue only by your eye.
It has to be your lie,
That we belong to anyone.
Where in this dream
I find I need your cry… much more than
your presence.
It's this, that I'm alive.

R&R:

Through eyes indescribable,
the world is in shambles;
    the reapers hand
        in every stroke of sight
    holds sympathy,
        invariably.

    Like an embers essence
        screaming color
            in smoke,
        so too does she breathe.

Shouldn't I?:

She remembered; she'd
always been dead.
A single step forward
tied the rope,
congratulated gravity,
just an inch.
A wetted hairs width
trigger trembles;
blood bellows in sweat
with screams like
a leaking faucet.
She remembers she's already dead,
and she asks why she shouldn't continue
on this river flooded red.

Because, I'd follow you.
To know a world like this has killed a light
so soft and kind and warm and bright,
is to know there's nothing here left for
me
to know.
I'd follow you into the river Styx,
to melt and merge with what ever
comes before and after this.
Do not leave me here
alone.
Do not leave, at all.

Waiting on the womb:

You were so old,
and I was just a dream.
intangible in touch, having me, just a beam,
as a neuron in your heart, beating pulse into reality.

Let it beat, and put on quite the fit,
your machine made of meat, I intend you use it.

Mother, and father, source of all that I am,
in thought, in touch, in all that I'll stand.
You were me first,
when I was just a thought.
Building, bridging death back to life;
In existence I fought.
Flowing backwards
from what was, to what is.

From what will only ever be;
from a beam, from a dream,
from you,
to me.

You Were Cloud Nine:

I've thought about fucking you
like an addict

licks the glass
clean.
I
Need a new drug
to hug and kiss
the outline

of my bones,
and mystify my nose
with pheromones,
that make me fall asleep

at night with thunderstorms
of dreams.

Consideration:

If I had a boy,
I would tell him to embrace his
invincibility…
                      and
romance mortality
in this journey,
                      but
not in the eyes of
another's identity…
                            because
although the curls of their lips
could kiss a twist upon your world
and energy, and
sway the tides of hues in skies
you once thought were so empty,
                                  they'll
destroy you.
They'll annihilate your entirety,
and you'll still
wish
you could love them more.

Juxtaposition:

October meets November, and
they're in love.
My… how they're in love –

It was never up to one
or
the other;
they could hardly stand a year away.
NO!
Not a month, nor a week,
but they will only ever be
but a day apart.
Neon filaments of florescent
hues and flakes.
A decorative littering
of yards and lakes.
A finger print from two,
a season within seasons,
An art.

The happiest seasons are the ones
In-between them.
Without a name,
or set forecast of rules
for branches withered
or drooled;
no wind dialed to a certain hymn.
Nothing but the slight progression
of one stage,
to the next.

A change, a love, resonating my bones,
and casting against the parameters
of my skin, a hex.
Because it's the change that chances discovering,
a merging of past to present,
and a curiosity our soul never forgets.

Hike:

I ate the sun today,
today,
today was morning dew.
I ate the sun like
summer rain,
and I still smell like you.

She sang to me:

She sang to me before we fell asleep
on sheets
of goals, and the chance of tomorrow existing.
The echo of her voice rippled on
into my dreams, in waves dissolving in scenes
christened by my dimethyltryptamine,
and a misfiring of electric strings.
The hectic collection works vigorously,
interpreting select symbols habitually
imprinted into itself throughout
our everyday lives,
to paint a picture of reality behind
my comfortably closed eyes.
All the while her voice played along;
in my life, I have sight, taste,
hearing and touch,
but above all else, and separate,
is her song.

Give Me One Good Reason Why I Shouldn't Die:

The one where you said you love
me.
The water,
       the thoughts,
              we don't see.
Flick the Bick and slaughter the shakes
with a remedy;
and still I never lie.
Why,
       why did you make me
              look you in
              the eye?
The webs we weave do tangle,
over time,
       and the loops are always present
in minds like yours and mine;
in Saturn's servants, in
       breathing life,
              in karma signs.
So, I'm afraid my dear, we were mostly
never alone…
       except for one loop we found,
all on our own…
A work of art – metaphysical with
       a medium of heart.
A moment of Zen I will never forget.
That when you're touching a river,
you're touching the first that is to come,
and the last that will
ever be.
So, I followed you. I followed you into it.

Smoke:

Like a fire which moves me,
the instinct of
heat, capable of remorse,
and sparks of delusions,
deliberate towards divorce and conclusions.

Flames can't end if they never truly started,
the thoughts that acid burn bends around
the light and soft hearted –
any consummation created
with intentions whole heartedly set to love,
is a dedication to a dream made of smoke.
An illusion of your hands catching a cloud.
I'm afraid no matter how strong, or how loud
your pupils could pound,
it will always be a fallacy.
Just a journey…
From a place within your mind,
to a new reality,
until you become lost alone,
in awe
of the new night sky.

Many of the stars we see,
unmoved of bright night,
cease to exist at the source of their light.
How do we know
who's alive,
or who's dead?

It all happens *SO* fast,

and on such a *grand* scale,
we never get the chance to really know anything.

Yet at the same
               time
                            we age like eon cells with
                            lifetime proteins. The
                incinerating light of our stars
        roast seams of mistake cries, drunk dialed at
a midnight hour. Seams of "I miss you" letters
written in dreams, and tossed into a sea of
consciousness. Cracks of polaroid
flowers now dead, that were
once so tremendously
vibrant and loved.

Love,
like the force of gravity between our island
and Andromeda
swims in the same spaces between our lips;
two and a half million
light years,
ago.

Cork Steam:

I hate being crossed,
but you sure hold your scotch.
And I hate this crown –
The being ups, and then downs.
But there's nothing around for me to faint
This niche.

    People,
        are puzzle leaches.
            They suck you dry, and
            leave you high
        to pick up all the pieces.
While I,
I introduce myself as
        revenge.
"A bomb lay," a good binge,
    a quick fix that never sticks;
a mind to make you cringe…

So then,
it isn't long before it's gone,
and you couldn't have ever cared;
    my personalities a pawn, so

I was never   really there.

Been Better:

You couldn't lose –
not yet again –
so, you tore off all your shredded skin
and wore the pain I poured
within my tainted mask
of hate,
        of sin,
so you could keep me
in the end.
        So, who are *you*?
            Where did this begin??
Will there ever truly be
        an end;
            I'll serve as a
reminder
            of what you
could've been;
        what might've came in a
package
        less fitting.
        To stay so steadily approaching, only
to   never
        reach you, this dream.
Carried softly across every yearning night.
I will never come true,
        never again,
and you
will live
with that until
you die.

Diary of a Mistress Slave:

What makes me sick
   Is I've ***BEEN*** loved.
Oh,
I've **HAD** love

      and I'm

             chained

instead,

      to

you.

Hurricane:

I will never love freely.
Not without glass invading my skin.
Not without a firm grip around my throat,
my tongue,
our wrists,
your lung.
I want nothing more than
twist apart your
kaleidoscopic ropes of heart
and intertwine.
I want, if nothing else,
to *love*.
To love you freely,
my dreary little ocean wave gone blind.
I died today, and
I'll never be free of this infinitum within
each breath you take.
So, love me freely, like a branch you break
in summers end,
as kindling for your storm.

Nurture:

Spoken like the *rain*,
her thoughts collect in puddles on our
soles.
With phonetics of tornados,
her voice,
it *shakes* in quakes of earth,
and in each breath, rests

black holes.

She doesn't say
she loves my laugh.
She wastes no comfort on
my hearts commotion.
She
does no battle, against
my souls' wrath.
She simply is
the nature of
my emotion.

A crown of storm clouds, and
Jewels of lightning.
A frown of acid rain,
Paint thunder screams soul
frightening.
A smile from the sun; oh love,
what have I done?
Where have your trumpets gone?
A smile for hours in moments

once ours and now
we're on the run.
Snow bank stares and
blizzard flares will my vision
"flee."
It isn't fair, but I
can't
care much for this weather;
she never gave a fuck about me.

...

Do not stay inside an electrified cage of barbed wire
and baton swings. The robot needles of emotion
solutes,
the venom brain washing powdered waters and
        foods; the pressured violation of
    insecurities on either side of the knife.
Do not stay inside a dynamic of lion eyes
    and coyote shivers.
     If this message
        reverberates
           under the parameters
          of your skin
           like a tornado
           ravages across
            stagnant
            planes,
           dear,
              flee.

Motivated Embers:

Don't take this as an insult
But
You're a beautiful tragedy.

You are someone who has
manifested suffering into
something of an art.
magically molding, redirecting,
refining what it is,
by downloading a world to be felt
into me.
A warlock of words,
A daemon of soul,
With the spirit of wolves.

Howl, howl your anguish,
your torture,
your vision of repair;
howl it to us, my creature
of art.

Holy Spirit Guardian Angel:

There is nothing fundamentally
good about this world,
               or the lives that it holds.
There is no such thing as good,
only distraction.
"Men love to save whores, son.
       It's a gross axiom.
       It's why people love the Jesus – Mary
story. Don't be a martyr, don't do it."

The gashes laugh against my chin.
       Always a little too late,
              and a couple hundred short.
"I think the lesson here is,
       don't save the whore,
              don't cum into shirts,
                  and
                      see a priest."

Polar Bear:

No one's ever inspected the vessel;
like a pup
       with a coat,
              I've designs
       across my chest.
       Manuscripts within my flesh,

       each row contouring a shadow
and of the faintest
              deadest line
that no one's ever cared
              to know.
Everything is a performance when
you don't know yourself.

    Change.

It is the only constant. We ride wind waves
of seasonal mental health,
like a pack of wolves;
we're not afraid
of your bear.

All the different versions of
'I' in howls and yelps,
all the different persons our eyes
stroke of sight's felt…
              I may have never been *you*,
but I've been *there*,
and I'll still be here
if it helps.

Phase:

Look at all these fine examples
of romanticized
love.
The honeymoon phase only lasts as long as
a few of the moons. The cycle continues:
Sunk Cost Fallacy and fear leaves us
bound
in stagnant, murky doubts. Where algae boils like
green living tar, and secrets moan beneath polluted
water.
        What ever year, what ever current date, it's
the afterlife of safe and sound. Our tears of fate that
sneeze calamity; the allergies and groans of
romance sounds
-the alarms-
as expectations are not kept.
As ghouls sprint out of where the forest lies
with machetes and spears; as venom spews forth
through the air, rocketed by
the subtlest of glancing contempt; your present
past
and future are
days only spent to be over wept. Where suddenly
you must
miss what you had,
had you,
had you had
seen it was more than enough, you wouldn't need to
want more now.

The Nurses Still Born:

Roll my eyes in on their keeper,
viewing prisoned time in past.
Stalking gates to those who weep her,
those whose home was shown at last.

She is mother, and tomb, and home.
She is where her children roam.
And so, I crept along to see
my own reflection,
distorted in time;
choked this infant here before me
and watched it sin immortal crime.

Watched it die some more inside,
closed its gates for the first night.
I watched its soul and its divide,
perhaps it left me out of freight?
Come to me then out of hiding
a lonely spirit guiding,
"Your weakness is in strength,
Your freedom found in fear.
Carry this in length,
As reason to be here."

So crying
and mourns of wombs
trapped dying
in the catacombs
of fluid light, that merge
the souls of those who's lost…
Who chase their purge from mothers' womb

And break free from their host.

Swimming, clawing
climbing, gnawing
bashing, hitting
splitting, pawing
screaming, stretching
rolling, diving
slipping, mixing
…dripping, flexing.
Trying to find their way back home…

So jealously watch her children,
while they aimlessly wonder blind,
on her vast egg in vacuum matter,
nestled on her electric wall.
BUT *YOU*…
being;
some kind of spirit
Some god
Some force
that which you opened to me and,
this little star of time, a gift you passed over me;
I'm gonna let it shine and guide me safely on my way
back home…

Safe Raven:

I asked her, "what is love?"
    She
        sighed.
"oh, I don't know… you can't put a
    label on 'it,' you know?
I hate this question; next question."

We laughed the rest of the night. Sparrows,
sparrows in the wind of time; her eyes said, *my
dear, I'm not gon'na be here too long. I'll try to
give you what you need.*
    Her eyes were ravens' claws. Like smoke
through cloth do our memories
        bleed through me, and
   I pray for you too…
a most evolved of birds,
hovering over a broken bones hue;
a hue that reads, *my dear, I'm not gon'na be here
too long, but I'll always be here for you.*
    Of this vapor mist and stench, I beg our past
remains.
        A love that I both pleasure
            never miss remains,
                for a friendship to have
                      that I could only ever
            wish.

5
The Humankind

Connected:

I've seen the machine, inside and apart
of
the spite, and deemed stupid
with confidence.
I've gleamed on the path where so many go
astray; force fed dead end jobs by day,
struck by fear when it's time to play,
and driven back until their pay.

I've seen the machine of pleading for love,
and doves above your selfish bleeding
crown…

I've seen the machine, and I want nothing
more than to turn myself around.
-
It's not the sadness from within that makes
you groan to go home, it's the sadness in
everyone else to prone the catalyst of feeling
alone…
that you're here to help, and yet you cannot.
No matter how much you sought to lift the
spirits of the beloved, it's them and them
alone who can bring themselves above it.

Now you're worthless in the sense of authenticity;
trapped in a glass box filled with everyone
else's poisonous misery,
and you
    try
so god damn hard not to breathe…

to disconnect from a world
born to bleed.
You strain to keep the red
from filling
your face and lungs
and screams…
but you breathe.

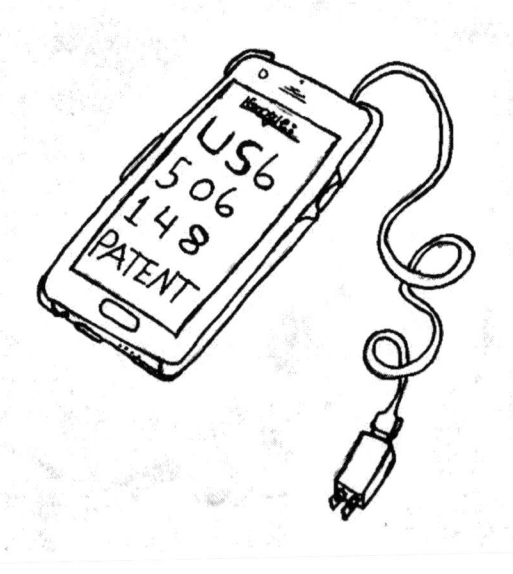

A Jolly Season:

I'm too broke for Christmas this year...
so instead I'll point out, how
it's a commercialized holiday
that's hypnotized an entire culture
into irrationally consuming the market,
per tradition,
thus, replacing the original traditional values,
which most people assume are Christian based,
but were actually robbed and raped
from pagan societies
as an attempt to convert as many of them as
possible to Christianity.
I'll point out this horror,
until I have enough money
to blindly follow this assigned duration
of a
societal masquerade of charity,
...
in hopes to ease and purge the guilt I've been buried
in throughout the other parts of the year,
by my family and friends,
and by my own inertly selfish,
cruel,
and unusual existence.

hopefully next Christmas I'll do better.

To Puppet Strings:

You breathe.
Two eyes in a sphere,
surrounded by a comet tails
contrasting mirrors; yin
and yang,
in a water droplet on a summer day
as it begins its ascension.
An evolution,
and evaporation
from the green valley where
children play with payments of their soul.
Tickets and coins of priceless imagination,
spent to deliver the determination to the *rest*
of
their
lives.
Lives where they'll, at a certain point, forget
about love and fun, to focus
on what's "right" or "wrong."
What's "true," or "false."
And whether or not it really means life…
if it doesn't have a pulse.

it:

The
>	homeless
>	shameless
>	*worthless*.
The "I don't know how to do this"
Stuck in a one mind
track
never open to listen
because the worlds already *raped* them of all the *facts*

pit in a hole
>	degenerative,
>	no good,
>	could have been ***asshole***
only offered up his own ***shit***
because
out of all of life
that's all he had of *it*.

Tick:

What is a mite?
Unapologetic little arachnid;
this fright –
set amongst a world on fire
with life,
and told to *chew…*
            chew…
                      chew…
and to survive, like the architecture
and designs
it feasts upon do.
And how scared are we
to hear the *shrieks*
that upon seeing a mite releases
in us;
but
what is a mite…

what is a mite, but a mite?

My Will:

I am a good person…
        At heart…
I was young…
                I didn't *know* any better.
I hurt,
        A lot,
For what I did to you,
and
            I'm sorry.

As authentically, unapologetically honest as I can be, from
        the bottom of my heart,

please, forgive me.

Celebrating the presidential election:

Happy day! Happy day,
where everybody gets a say!

Pick your suits of ace, or spades
and chose the one to lead our way;
to burn in hell or drown in Hades.

And if it's rigged, to our dismay,
we'll play our hands out *anyway*!
The pot has thinned,
the plot has thickened…
For this to end
our <u>chants</u> have quickened!
And then again come next November,
emptied by elected louse,
We'll all look back to say "remember,
No one ever beats the house."

      Cheers.

Deforestation:

There's crying.
Heavy wheezing and humming
likened to bulldozers
running
and I hear it inside
every hair on my arm.
The stench of them burning
whimpers through the
gaps of my teeth;
inhaled
of this male charm. I
suffocate a thousand times
beneath the run
the sprint
the flee and flight.
I survive with all
my will and might
but not all are meant
to race the flames.
Or the drums of the engines.
Their metal claps like penetration
in my lobe,
my brain.
Timber towed beneath
my gums
like splinters burrowed
and sheathed
for fun -
I've no connection to this death
of smothered air
other than that I care…

and that's all that I can do.
I care.

Sex Work:

Perhaps physical illness is a fallacy;
a calling from a thought, ruling
in the catacombs
of us walking tomb stones,
who won't or can't accept infinity
while we're punching
in the clocks.
It's thought,
in confidence telling
consciousness that it isn't free…
maybe, maybe…
       maybe that's what makes
it so hard to breathe. Perhaps that's why
       your bones and joints
             ache.
That's why we squint under the sun to see...

you must give what you take,
there's a push just to pull.
You consume what you make,
buying time with your soul.

Fucking for *fuck's sake*,
and surviving to grow old.
Paying just to be,
kid,
your souls already sold.

Conspirator:

What other choice did I have Doctor? I'm a mess.
A citizen unfit for society. . . Ha, *society*. I hate the term now.
I was never very social anyway,
but a society? All it means now is
a system of parasitic worker ants in
the form of drones,
programmed to program themselves with
shit. After all it is called a "television program,"
isn't it?
Of course, the psychopathic queen bee
of each society
eventually takes her own shit on
ninety nine percent
of what those drones program themselves with.
    it keeps us entertained that way… to run in
circles, and forget each lap.
What's clean is what's left, and what's left
in one's and zero's
is never good for the drones.
Because, what do they know?
How could they know what's good for them?
That psychopathic bitch at the top doesn't know
anything either.

No one does.

So, it's just one big carnival circus act,
a bunch of monkeys on a wild,
bloody,
orgy filled,

goose chase.
It's all chained together too doctor, all of it.
Tied like a web made of poison and *fucking lies*.
These assholes aren't even *trying*.
The educational system ties back to the banks and oil companies
who control the economy and our government,
which controls its citizens with an armed bureaucracy
and theft,
plus, pharmaceutical company drugs,
funded by the companies that make *poisons*,
which also fund the farms that give us our food.
Poisons Doc; the poisons that go into pesticides and cigarettes and chemicals they used to use in war before the UN banned them.
They're funding our *medicine*, and our *food*.
So, us,

"*citizens*"

are first molded by this educational system,
created by the banks,
for the banks.
And then spit out into a cum stained shit filled unapologetic *social experiment*.
That's what society is, an experiment. Have you seen
the technology? We don't know what we're doing to ourselves – to our *children*. We're
watching it happen, just
hoping
for the best…

Perspective:

In our veins runs the blood of our ancestry.
From the anthropoid mammalian ape, to the
predecessor of wolves,
                              to the giant reptilians
                       that stampeded their bones
      into our Earth,
to the vegetation that nearly
microscopic organisms once consumed.
You're the product of a 4.54-billion-year long
planetary evolution, we've deemed
                         the personification
and alias,
"nature."
In it is the timeless pulse of consciousness,
and its various levels, wherein you happen to
fall on the rippling wave of sentience.
                            Quite
An evolution, indeed –
The inanimate
becoming animated.
Animal to humanoid.
Humanoid to
personhood.
From small, to grand,
to cosmic scales.
Becoming things
      from things
      we hailed, and
continue to hail; life.
       From dust, to dust,
              our planetary spec…

I want to go home:

I was never a risk, not much a chance taker;
always had a say as "no,"
not much a life dancer.
Never a savior, for I was too afraid to conquer,
thus from fear I was unsaved.
Awaken, laughing, they say,
at how lifeless was the life we lived in the dreams we weaved.
As for me, I awaken without intent to remain in either ether or plasma,
for I fit in neither,
other than in short spurts of waves of will,
that which I do not own.
A ray of light which only mirrors, in smoke and steam,
in fluidic air,
oscillating with vibrations emitted from your voice which *defines me.*

What it is in me you see; ultimately
each expression of me, from you, is a reality
waiting to be dubbed true
from us two.
I am your threshold, your gateway,
a neuron, our pulse,
your code that, if by will, will allow you to let me be;
until so I am imprisoned as you, me, and the infinite in 3.

Allow me please, to rise as the sun,

to pass over your eye, to kiss your skin, your soul,
and allow me then to set,
to release,
relieve,
breathe
and end.

Human Animal:

Individuality is a fallacy.
You don't want to experience
raw humanity.
It's broken – rapid while
shallow,
       insecure,
              afraid,
                      ugly.
Quick to leap
out and latch onto
anything, in which will play with the
fractures of a fizzling state.

What's real
is better left
unseen.

6
Rising sun

The Observer:

Ridden by metacognition;
adventure is medicine.
A distraction of our meta-sins,
masquerading as heaven.
Eden is a cold creek, Eden
is a card game. Eden is
the
trans-placental message
our mother culture's eaten.
We can witness God,
                sex,
                      and Satan;
we can witness backs broke, scarred, and beaten.
                We can witness
                      and
                                that's all that
we can do.

We don't ask for life, or love –
for nights kissed with cocaine, chemical doves, and
acid rain.
        We don't always see the sighs,
the sun sets, setting our world
ablaze.
I'm afraid of future light and endless days,
shredded of their mortality.
I don't want to be forever;
I don't want this dead reality.

THIS IS NOT A PIECE OF WRITING:

This
is a PICTURE.
With layers
and *layers* of <u>paint</u>; of *all* the colors of the
rainbow…
and mistakes of shading, relentlessly enduring the
effort and time *bled* into
every pore and pimple crater
of this canvas.
It's relying to you
a **MASTERPIECE** of a beautiful landscape
with waves of terrain
and texture,
radiantly contrasting colors that convey their own
natural battle;
all of it reminding you of the gust of wind
that almost picked you off your feet
when you were just a little bit younger.

and in the corner, is your signature.

Death is not dying (riding the spiral):

It is not your last breath,
whether it was torn from the space around you,
or entered delicately as a final pull.
It is not the cooling of your flesh,
nor the boiling shocks to your brain,
as it attempts to register and analyze,
perpetually.
It is not the burning bridge to those you love,
the ones you leave behind to beg
for your return within their dreams and memories.
It certainly is not the last word that brushes your
upper lip,
as it quivers to flaccidity,
traveling vigorously with energy into our air.
It is not the end of your reflection, encoded by those
conveying your image of them;
your idea, your figment of a dream, whether light or
sound.
It's not what you left in your name, as an
indentation of existence on earth,
like the finger print of the soul that inhabited you.
It's not the battle scars you left on others hearts; the
stains on the grass from the tears
you once sucked out.
It will never be the way out of the pain you feel
now; from the way you groan, wrapped in bed
at night, begging to know why… why are you here?
Death's a journey to travel, just like you

whether you're aware or not.

Chant:

Time will know me, and
all my pretty little itch – scratch;
leaving flies to a lion.

Of a choreographed hive,
              of what plan, could this plane devise,
that we're all on good terms from a distance?
        Of what end warrants a beginning?

I can't feel

That this world is anymore.
I'm sheltered behind false names.
I'm cold and
animal
inside; my eyes
can't handle this terrain.
But nonetheless, time will know me.
              I've died to make it so.
                  It's better time,
          my soul enclose,
      than for I to hold it
in a grave that no one ever knows.

Scriptures:

mirror full of memories,
pixels paint our pictures.
God becomes a tragedy, and
desktops full of friends become
our scriptures.
The worlds so small and odd.
Full of cycles and chapters,
refusing you a life ordinarily
mediocre.

To see magic, just remember to
see. magic.
Just remember that there's echoes
in the cosmos, and knowledge
in the never.
That our dreams go on without us,
and *nothing* lasts forever.

You were never something all along,
and all along we dance to Lunas' silver,
piercing song;
all along Saturns' rings, and sing
in breaths of right and wrong.
So that we may learn the lessons;
answers to questions forgotten so…
so long…
Over and over and over and over and over and over
and over and over and over and over and over and
over and over and over and over and over and over
and over and over and over and over and over and
over and over and over and over and over and over

and over and

2:51 AM:

The transition from life to death is perpetual,
long, and weary.
Like a log fire being eaten to ashes,
where the flames are the spirit, soul, and
consciousness,
and the wood is the body.
At its peak, all that arrests anyone's attention is the
flame,
but as it descends, the ashes become the art.

The 'smoke' is what I identify with.
The smoke is the passage of time, in that
it's the experience it emits, like light and warmth,
but it's
intangibly bound to slip through our fingers.
It's the levels of our existence we can't
consistently beware of, while holding onto
ourselves.
It's elusive and passing even to the source of its
emitter.

Then there's the feeling of an unsettling, uneasy,
incessant and growing sense of "wrong,"
the kind of feeling you get in your gut when
randomly you've a premonition that something
horrible is about to happen.
Like a lingering entity of shadow on every
surface and wall around you.

Then higher still, a level of nonexistent existence
and paradoxical gnosis that people can only ever

feel for a moment until it collapses on itself and wipes the whole slate clean…
Running back and forth in this awareness is like how
our being breathes… in and out, the form of our soul.
Which if that's the case, mines having a panic attack.

(3:12 AM) goodnight… have fun.

A Nondeterministic Nihilist I Once Knew:

Could you *fucking try*?!
Pull a lie,
twist the truth
cry tears to fill the room to roof –
I gloom the day you say
"I don't care."
Express an opinion! *FIND* a feeling
to share.
SHARE!
I keep cutting and peeling back another layer of
skin,
to sell out my soul
for the hole I live in.
You're out of excuses,
I'm dried of emotion from
this lame games abuse
of who's eyes are more sunken.

I don't care about how much you don't care!
What about what you do?!
DO YOU??
Is it *possible* of you?
Are you compatible with the idea
of formulating one?

What comes of this acceptance of nothing?
…. Are you comfortable with that?

Blind:

What a loop of chaos. Order.
Chaos. Order.
How much it burns when I don't play
with fire. Oh, how
much I suffer without
my game of suffering.

A fly weaves a web to catch the spider
who consumes him.
The bass draws a line with a hook
made of gold, and power, and sex,
and drugs, and a legacy.
How
empty should you be
to survive anything?
Justice dances first world,
as it watches angels
rape and genocide children.
American rats eat snakes, and argue
in tongues of prosperity.
Liquefy what's left and drip it
In the corner

of your eye. For the night
is better seen, when the whole
world's gone blind.

Some of us:

Some of us have scars on our memories,
Callused and risen above the
Surface of our persons
Personalities.

The humans, the kids who don't always feel so human;
who prefer the cover of soft nights
and rain
and the collars of our coats;
the dancers of a choreographed night
of cracking fire and crickets chirping
under stippling starlight and
open ended sentences…

      We hold on to what hurts.
    What beats away and just doesn't
know
how to stop.
      We hold on because
we've *found* something that can *still hurt*;
and we will *stay alive* knowing that

        we still have that in us.

The Puzzle:

Our world is on fire.

THIS. This is all naturally
Hell.
Fire like *screams*, and weary
                             Fears.
Eruptions of sulfur, love, and
       Cool soot *anger*
               Magma tears drip coals
of   failure.
     And thick. Black. Smoke. Numbs
Our sense of danger.
               Our basic form of existence,
                   is agony,
And our only escape is heaven;
if only for moments.
               But the folklore
                   And white light
     can't sugar coat the gates
or all that is temporary.

Angels for Eyes:

Angels spectate in every
superposition,
arresting our consciousness
from the outer envelope of our dimension;
receiving experience –
lust, love, hatred, pain, trust, envy, sorrow, vain,
for there is no room for humanity in Heaven.

Eyes along the myelin sheath of
our fourth dimension, retaining our
electric wreath in purest intention.
We will indeed become God, like
It with us, through an
endlessness of
reiteration.

We each have two angels,
and a third source of creation.

Roots:

Crushing willows willing eyes to breathe their image
of might; every strand
and string
of green delight. Every wisp
of wind to dream this slate of reality in motion.
This elixir time, a soulful potion,
revealing moments of lucid emotion, in us,
our mother willow tree. This dripping *grace*, this
joyous being, with secrets only stars could gleam.
This ancient bark and soil incents – delivering me full
contentment, that it is here, and so am I.
It is here, and so
Am I.
Then as it grows then so will I, and
as it goes then so I'll die.
This mighty being beyond me, before me does
it lay its heavy thicket head, whispering
reminders once – **I AM ALIVE.**
As long as the wind strokes through her hair,
as long as light flashes in my eyes,
as long as the image holds in my mind, I…
I
Am
Alive.
        If only for a moment, and for moments
at a time, and in this moment this weeping willow finds
the reapers widow to shake her withered hand.

I'm connected to death, like she connects me to her land.
Though arrested by both her gaze and grip, I feel
That I'm a life.
Just for a moment she breathed to me her mission,
natures religion, her clarity of strife.

Answers:

An ego-dead room, with full black carpet
littered in velvet stars…
and in an entire space
swims ultraviolet waves. Plumes of cloud
and technicolored noise
of a live world,
racing about…
swirling around.
Cumulative collections of experience,
of parables, and ideas,
strung together above my head
and cemented to the ground.
My dear malleable, breathing world,
aware and upside down,
where is the path that I walk now?
without gravity,
without a solid
standing
reality.

The path of unsure, inconsistent fluidity.
The cobble stone of a questionable life,
inside a queered and criminally
bombarded mind.
I find vacation, in this holiday like time.
I find the nostalgia bridges
hope,
like boredom bridges crime.
I find that I am most familiar
with the parts of me
that are not mine.

Luke's Code:

Everybody dies;
not everybody truly lives.
As for me,
I'll live forever
and die while trying;
death is sane
and sanity doesn't exist.
Thus, insanity is a creation of itself.

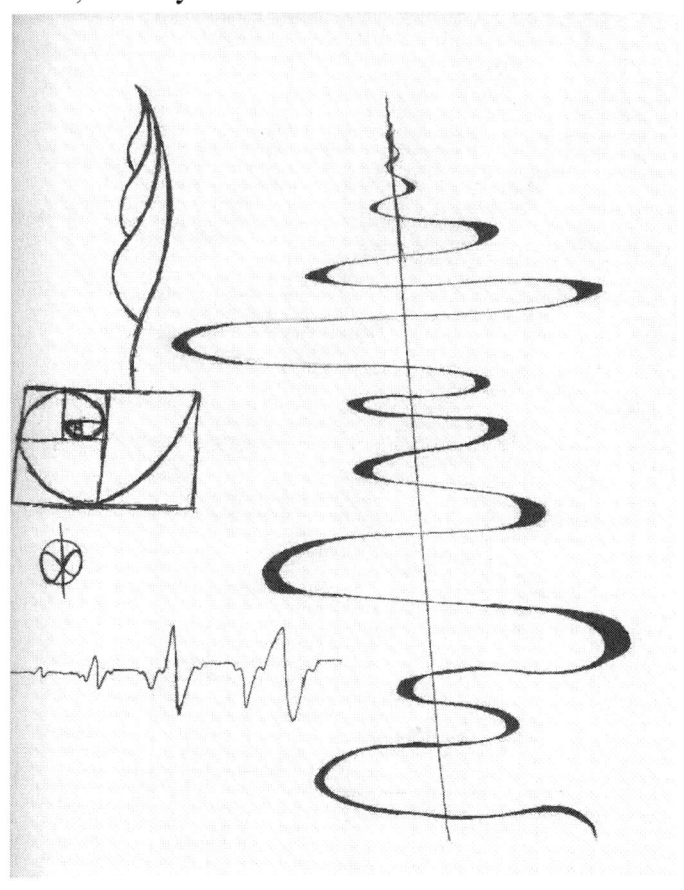

Anthem:

Try to dream, dream of the corpses at the dining room door.
If you listen closely you can almost hear their thin mistakes echo,
like an ocean in a shell. A whores name I wear, the name I wear
When I'm a whore, and of thoughts breath I breathe no more.
For in deaths light the nights no more;
…
I drink my secrets to the floor.
I drink these pills and lies and hills of time and *all* these words I drink to climb until I climb no more.
For life's another truth to find,
Somewhere behind – before the dining room door.
Before she opens her stalagmite jaw agape.
Before of more you cannot take and you blow your brains across the bedroom –
Wait! There's more to pick at, at this open sore.
I'm conscious mostly of unconscious horror, and the terror it takes to
Cut your chest and spill your guts for others sake
And say "I'M ALIVE, GOD DAMNIT, I AM ALIVE"
And say it loud and proud almost like you mean it.
"I AM ALIVE" almost like it's starting to feel alright;
"I am alive."

Dimensions of the Astral Plane:

We see in fragments of the 3D, reconstructed
and
perceived fourth dimensionally.
Of the space-time reality, we peak behind the
curtain of the fifth, aware of the teeming
possibilities.
What would you be doing right now, if
you weren't reading this book?
What could you have done different, yesterday –
what will be done tomorrow… are you sure?

And it isn't until we're outside of it that we
feel weightless. The nirvana birth
of leaving
the body. The absence of cool, or warm,
and past or future or
present at all, all thawed and wasted away
with the collection of experience you once called
your life… but remember as vaguely
as a dream. Where
even though right now,
it is all that is, sensitive and urgent,
in this plane, you're perfectly content
without knowing
what it means. For now, you are awake. Up, and
moving about, surrendering naturally to a
gravity of what's unknown, but familiarly a foreign
home.
It's here that within the two planes of time
and possibility, you find
the astral plane of serenity.

Life Flashed Before Our Eyes:

Just think; it could be tonight.
It could be tonight just as much
as any other night. All
we ever do is pass on; life is the dying process,
but we don't control the winds that push
us through.
Not until we tie the ropes into
a noose and cut the sails,
to sway and bob alone at sea.
And what a world,
or mind,
and ocean would we appear
to see…
and what nerve of we to
come into the dreams of evermore.
Coming here, the stolen fruit of
release, only to regurgitate
the frame of beast we
strived so hard to
ponder, then leave…
only to ponder it once more
again, slightly different,
only glimpsed familiarity,
only knowing we should
and shouldn't repeat.
Death is the thunder following
our final strike.
Death is the howling
of wolves,
upon our moonlight.

The Birth Rest of a Grave Stone:

        This is
             not
      what you are;
            this is
      where you begin;
            this is
      what you might feel…

About the author:

Emenual Wolff is a Michigan based poet, author, artist and performer. His poetry pivots around a metaphysical philosophy of existence with a nihilistic skew. He engages in themes such as morality, religion, insanity, society, love, addiction, psychology, mortality, and the nature of life, death, and reality. In sharing these writings with the world, he hopes to place his readers beside themselves, in a space both familiar, and unknown. This, he suggests, allows for a frame of mind that's beyond itself. Between writing and creating art, Emenual Wolff is traveling venues delivering spoken word and promoting the benefits of reading over watching television, as well as the protection of honey bees. You can find more on Emenual Wolff at: www.emenwritings.webs.com

:@emenwritings   :@earthisanisland